INSIDE JOB

Published by CelebrityPress™, Orlando, FL
A division of The Celebrity Branding Agency®

Celebrity Branding® is a registered trademark
Printed in the United States of America.

ISBN: 9780985364366
LCCN: 2012939049

This publication is designed to provide accurate and authoritative information with regard to the subject matter covered. It is sold with the understanding that the publisher is not engaged in rendering legal, accounting, or other professional advice. If legal advice or other expert assistance is required, the services of a competent professional should be sought. The opinions expressed by the authors in this book are not endorsed by CelebrityPress™ and are the sole responsibility of the author rendering the opinion.

Most CelebrityPress™ titles are available at special quantity discounts for bulk purchases for sales promotions, premiums, fundraising, and educational use. Special versions or book excerpts can also be created to fit specific needs.

For more information, please write:

CelebrityPress™
520 N. Orlando Ave, #2
Winter Park, FL 32789
or call 1.877.261.4930

Visit us online at www.CelebrityPressPublishing.com

INSIDE JOB

Contents

FOREWORD

By Dr. Tom Orent

Dentists. Who are they? Where did they come from?! It's likely you've never given a second thought to these questions. Yet understanding who they are and just *why* they chose to become dentists may give you a deeper appreciation for *your* dentist the next time you visit.

I was struck by what Edwin Land (founder of Polaroid) said about Steve Jobs. Jobs was "at the intersection of humanities and science." In Jobs' biography, Walter Isaacson reports that in reference to Land's comment, Jobs remarked, "I like that intersection. There's something magical about that place." Hearing this brought me four decades back into my past, when as a young teenager I'd made up my mind... I was destined to be a dentist. We share Job's passion for that intersection of humanities and science.

What inner burning desires drive dentists' lifelong pursuit of the art and science of dental medicine? My window into the mind of dentists goes beyond my personal experience as a practitioner. As a national provider of post-doctoral continuing dental education I've had the opportunity to work with thousands of dentists from all over the world. The majority of dentists share a number of common traits.

We are driven to continual learning to the point of obsession. Good enough is *never* good enough. We strive for clinical results which in many cases far exceed the "bar" or standard that you as a patient may expect of us. We love to help people. We spend our careers at that intersection described by Edwin Land, blending the art and science of dental medicine with our yearning to help our fellow man.

Dentistry has evolved more over the last two decades than the previous seventy-five years combined. Our knowledge, care, skill and judgment have blossomed unlike anything we could have dreamed of back in our days at the university. Recent research has opened our eyes to the myriad of ways that dental medicine and your dental health are inextricably interwoven with whole body health. Adverse conditions in the mouth can have far-reaching deleterious consequences on your overall health. Research has highlighted the link between oral diseases and Heart Disease, Stroke, Diabetes and problematic pregnancies just to name a few.

Your dentist is an artist, a scientist and a dedicated health practitioner as well as a humanitarian. I am thrilled to have the opportunity to write the foreword for this book as it gives me license to express just how proud I am to be involved in a collaborative effort with my fellow dentist-authors represented in the chapters to follow. Each and every one of the dentists you are about to meet in this book exemplifies leadership, compassion, devotion to service and the lifelong pursuit of professional excellence.

CHAPTER 1

The Oral-Systemic Connection –

New Science Warns About New Threats to Your Heart

By Gregory J Wych, DDS

As if you didn't have enough to worry about…new science has shown us that there is a link between the mouth and the rest of your body. This link has been termed the "Oral-Systemic Connection" and has caused dental professionals and physicians to rethink the relationship between oral health and the health of your body.

Today, people are living longer. Dentistry has improved the war against tooth decay. The increased use of fluoride, from the public drinking water, to supplementation and administration by dental professionals to our youth, has greatly decreased the incidence of tooth decay.

But Gum Disease has supplanted tooth decay as the leading problem in oral health. Gum disease is more properly termed "periodontal disease." The American Academy of Periodontology states that three out of four Americans have some sort of periodontal disease, ranging from mild gingivitis to more severe periodontitis.

THERE IS A WAR GOING ON IN YOUR MOUTH!

There are more than 300 different species of bacteria attacking your gums and teeth 24 hours a day, seven days a week.

It's really a perfect storm of a problem! A warm, moist environment, that is well fed, with sugars and acids, becomes a perfect incubator for growing the bacteria that cause us harm. The bacteria and their toxic by-products work themselves down around the teeth and into the gums, initiating an immune system reaction, which becomes a chronic source of infection and battleground. This inflammation locally causes the gums to become inflamed, and eventually the bone around the teeth starts to be destroyed. As this bone is lost, the teeth become loose, more difficult to clean, and the cycle gets worse and worse. Eventually this can lead to tooth loss.

Obviously, loose teeth (and lost teeth) are a bad enough problem. Chewing becomes more difficult, even painful. Everything from bad breath to indigestion and stomach problems can result. Even sleep problems!

But now, new science has shown that the inflammation in our gums does not remain limited to your mouth. Dangerous bacteria and inflammatory proteins are able to circulate freely in the bloodstream. And many of the "markers" for inflammation in your body are increased (worsened) by an increase in inflammation in your mouth.

WHAT IS CRP?

C-reactive protein is an acute phase protein produced by the liver. These acute phase reactant proteins rise dramatically during inflammatory processes occurring in the body. As it turns out, CRP significantly increases the chances of future heart attack or stroke by affecting blood vessels and creating blood clots. CRP is thought to be part of the body's early defense system against infections. Arterial damage occurs as a result from inflammation due to the chemical insults of CRP. So CRP can be considered a general marker for inflammation and infection and a general predictor for heart disease risk.

Research suggests that patients with elevated basal levels of CRP are at an increased risk for diabetes, hypertension and cardiovascular diseases. Other studies indicate that when you treat periodontitis, CRP levels go down. Heart attack survivors who suffer advanced periodontitis show significantly higher levels of CRP.

The American Heart Association recommends a CRP test only when a doctor is not sure whether to treat a patient at intermediate risk of heart disease. This is because a patient at low risk doesn't need treatment and a patient at high risk needs treatment, regardless of CRP levels. But some doctors recommend having a CRP test whenever you have your cholesterol checked.

A high CRP level predicts high risk, even if your cholesterol is low. CRP testing is needed to identify these individuals and motivate them to live healthier lives—stop smoking, start to exercise, and lose weight, all of which lower CRP levels and cardiovascular risk. The CRP test is simple enough. Your blood is drawn and sent to a lab for analysis. There has been some research on CRP testing and saliva levels, but the results have been shown to be less predictable.

The blood test alerts your doctor to the presence of inflammation. When inflammation is present anywhere in the body, the immune system increases production of infection-fighting white blood cells. These cells can infiltrate plaque deposits in coronary arteries and destabilize them so that they rupture, causing particles that can block an artery, thus causing a heart attack. Testing for CRP gives you an idea of whether the internal scenario set off by inflammation could be affecting your coronary arteries.

PERIODONTITIS AND HEART DISEASE

Studies confirm that dental health is significantly worse in people who have had an acute heart attack than in healthy people. A British study showed that poor oral hygiene and periodontitis both increased the risk of coronary heart disease by 25%. The same study showed the risk was 72% higher among men under the age of 50! People who have the markers for periodontal disease in their bloodstream ran a risk of heart attack that was two to four times higher than those who did not have periodontal disease. Other studies from Scotland to the United States have shown associations between deep periodontal and abnormalities in electrocardiograph readings. Elevated levels of inflammatory compounds that arise from periodontal disease cause significant changes in the lesions that lead to hardening of the arteries!

The American Heart Association has identified periodontitis as one of the major chronic infections that put you at a higher risk for atherosclerosis and coronary heart disease later in life. The AHA implies that oral infection (periodontal disease) causes a chronic inflammatory burden on the body's entire system. The AHA states that oral pathogens have evolved the capacity to directly invade tissues throughout the body, triggering inflammatory events that overburden other organs and systems. One of these pathogens, P. gingivalis, found commonly in the mouth has been found in the DNA of the tissues in diseased aortas and artery clogging plaques throughout the body. Whew!

Periodontitis has also been linked to ischemic stroke, the kind of changes that alter blood flow to the brain. Other studies link the cumulative effects of chronic periodontal disease, thickened carotid arteries, and stroke. So gum disease can be a good predictor of stroke. And since 75% of Americans have some sort of gum disease, and up to 30% may have severe periodontitis, you can do the math and see the potential problem.

WHAT ABOUT PREGNANCY AND GUM DISEASE?

Gum disease is not just linked to heart and stroke problems. Changing hormone levels in women during pregnancy can lead to flare ups of the disease. The primary risk of periodontitis during pregnancy is preterm delivery and low birth weights. Many types of infection have been associated with the risk of preterm delivery, including periodontal infections. The presence of periodontal disease at weeks 21-24 into pregnancy is associated with preterm delivery. Women with pre-existing periodontal disease in the second trimester have a 4.5 to 7 times greater risk of premature delivery. Another study showed that women who were treated for gingivitis (a mild form of gum disease) before their 28th week of pregnancy had a significantly lower incidence of premature birth. The study concluded that any oral infections, diagnosed during any time of pregnancy, must be treated as soon as possible.

GUM DISEASE AND DIABETES.

People with diabetes are more likely to get periodontal disease, a chronic infection in the gums inside the mouth. Research is now suggesting that the reverse may also be true: people with chronic gum infections may be more likely to get diabetes. Researchers recently looked at data from a large ongoing national health survey and found that people who had a chronic gum infection at the beginning of the survey study were more likely to get diabetes during the next 20 years.

A useful marker in the measurement of diabetes (Types 1 and 2) is HbA1c. In addition to random fasting blood glucose levels, HbA1c levels are routinely measured in the monitoring of people with diabetes. That is, the higher the glucose concentration in blood, the higher the level of HbA1c. On those occasions when blood glucose is high, the hemoglobin in the blood may be marked or "glycated". The percentage of the hemoglobin that is glycated is an indication of the patient's level of glucose (or blood sugar) control over the last two months. A value of less than 5.9% is normal, a value over 7% is typically considered diabetic, and 6%-7% is typically considered pre diabetic. Since periodontal bacteria in the bloodstream can increase blood sugar and A1c, treating the periodontal disease can reduce Hb-A1c and diabetes risk. It is important to note that periodontal disease can seriously impact one's ability to control his or her blood sugar. Research also shows that it is possible for elevated blood sugar to cause a pre-diabetic to become diabetic. The Hb-A1c test is only a screening test and more testing to include a fasting blood glucose test is necessary to confirm the presence of diabetes.

OTHER LINKS

Obesity has been a health problem and a risk factor for a number of diseases and longevity, and periodontal disease is no different. Overweight individuals between the ages of 18 and 34 show a huge correlation to periodontal disease. (Underweight subjects within the same age ranges were less likely to have periodontal disease.)

Periodontal disease has also been linked to chronic kidney disease. Those with periodontitis are twice as likely to have chronic kidney disease, and subjects with missing teeth were 85% more likely to have chronic kidney disease.

There have been other studies that have shown links between periodontitis and osteoporosis, ulcers, arthritis, lung disease and even cancer. There have also been secondary links between sleep apnea and snoring and periodontal disease.

PREVENTION AND TREATMENT
OF PERIODONTAL DISEASE

A common misconception amongst patients is that bleeding gums are normal. Bleeding gums are one of the best (or worst) signs of gum disease! Think of gum tissue as the skin on your hand. If your hands bled every time you washed them, you would know something is wrong.

Other signs of gum disease include red, swollen or tender gums, gums that have pulled away from the teeth, persistent bad breath, pus between the teeth and gums, loose or separating teeth (spaces start to open up between the teeth), a change in your "bite", or a change in the way crowns or partial dentures "fit".

The thoughts of "floss or die" are quite a bit over-exaggerated. There is quite a bit more than just "flossing" in the prevention and treatment of periodontal disease. Unfortunately, often the medications that many people must take can make patients susceptible to gum infections. These include antihistamines, antidepressants, cancer drugs, steroids and especially those that cause "dry mouth", disrupting the mouth's bacterial ecosystem. Genetic, microbial, immunological and environmental factors influence both the risk and progression of periodontal infection.

But do not despair! You are not doomed to periodontal disease… it can be controlled. And the therapies now are incredibly improved over the periodontal treatment of "the old days".

Traditional periodontal therapy usually started with a procedure called "Scaling and Root Planing", often referred to (semi-euphemistically) as "deep cleaning". Then, the dentist or specialist (periodontist) would surgically access the roots of the teeth and clean, shape and add bone to help support the teeth. The surgical access part of the treatment ("slicing the gums") was the portion that patients dreaded. And who wouldn't dread having their gums opened up with a scalpel and after cleaning and scraping, stitched or super-glued back together!

This mode of treatment, improved but essentially unchanged for decades, gave periodontal therapy a bad name. It worked very well, and still today is the standard of care for treating advanced gum disease.

But the recent development and utilization of LANAP has changed the way dentists and periodontists are treating gum disease. Actually this procedure was first pioneered in the early

1990's but has gained huge acceptance over the past five to seven years. LANAP stands for "laser assisted new attachment procedure" and is actually a trademarked name by a company that sells a type of dental laser used to treat gum disease. (Several other types of lasers can also be used to accomplish the same procedure.)

The laser has a special wavelength (1064 nm). Most dental lasers operate at different wavelengths that allow the dentist to do many things, from filling teeth to trimming gums, but are not appropriate for this type of procedure.

This special wavelength allows the dentist or periodontist to remove the diseased gum tissue, and any bacteria or calculus (tartar) that has attached to the root of the tooth, without damaging the root of the tooth. After the root surface and inner gum tissue (periodontal pocket) is disinfected and sterilized by the laser energy, the gum tissue is able to reattach to the root of the tooth, reducing the pocket depth. The supporting bone also increases in density.

After the procedure, which does not require any cutting or stitching of the gums (at most a little bit of cyanoacrylate is used to stabilize the gum tissue), most patients only need to take some ibuprofen (or similar NSAIDs) to relieve any minimal discomfort. The patient needs to be careful brushing, no flossing, for a couple of weeks.

The treating dentist monitors the patient closely, usually checking after a week, a month and then three months. Most times, after the procedure, the dentist will perform an "equilibration", which is some minor adjusting on the teeth so the patient does not bite too hard on some areas of the teeth, and with equal pressure throughout (this usually does not even require novocaine).

Typical results of LANAP (and similar procedures) are awesome! Eight year retrospective studies show a 50% reduction in gum pocket depths, and a 48% improvement in bone density.

LANAP and similar procedures are helping patients and taking the fear and dread out of the treatment of gum disease. *But the key to treating gum disease, and improving your overall health and well being is to not ignore the telltale signs.* <u>It could mean your life!</u>

About Dr. Greg Wych

Gregory J Wych DDS graduated from undergraduate school from Xavier University in Cincinnati, Ohio (1980) and Dental School from Case Western Reserve University School of Dentistry in 1984. Practiced in the US Navy from 1984-1987, stationed at Parris Island, SC (MCRD), Beaufort Naval Hospital, and Marine Corps Air Station, Beaufort, SC. Private practice in Irmo, SC since 1988, and most recently opened a dental office in the Vista area of downtown Columbia, SC. Owner of the South Carolina Children's Dental Group. Alumni of The Las Vegas Institute for Advanced Dental Studies, The Dawson Center for Advanced Studies, the Piper Educational Center, and the Seattle Institute for Advanced Dental Studies.

Member of the Visiting Faculty of the Spear Institute at the Scottsdale Center for Dental Studies and the Spear Study Club. Former Independent Business Advisor for the Glazer Kennedy Insider Circle. Member of the American Dental Association, Central District of the South Carolina Dental Association, and the Greater Columbia Dental society. Member of the American Academy of Cosmetic Dentistry, Member of the Give Back a Smile Foundation, the American Academy of Computerized Dentistry, Doctors of Conscious Sedation, Academy of Laser Dentistry International, American Implant Institute, Academy of Oral Medical Toxicology, and the American Association of Oral Systemic Health.

He was awarded "Small Business of the Year" by the Irmo Chamber of Commerce (for 2009). Advance training in sedation dentistry, cosmetic and comprehensive dentistry, implant dentistry, TMJ, botox, and dermal fillers and other esthetic procedures. Active member of St. Peter's Church in Columbia, South Carolina.

CHAPTER 2

TECHNOLOGY –
The Best Is Yet To Come

By Dr. Herbert Schneider

It only cost four cents. It took me three days to prepare for it. I thought that it was the best accomplishment of my life. It was the first Monday after Thanksgiving, I was six years old, and it was my first class trip. We were going to the post office and I was sending my masterpiece, my first letter.

This was not just any plain old letter. It was written on bonded paper – the kind that grown-ups use, and it had two complete sentences on it.

"Hi, my name is Herb. I am in first grade."

I printed those 2 lines carefully and neatly folded the full sheet of paper. I then placed it into the envelope and wrote the address on the front as dictated by my mother. I licked the flap and slopped my saliva over the four cent Abraham Lincoln stamp to make sure that it would stick. And now it was finished and ready to be mailed – to myself.

At the post office I waited on line with my other classmates until it was my turn. I stood on my tippy toes and handed the envelope to the postal clerk, who stamped it and then flipped it into a large bin, sending my letter on its journey.

The next few days after school I would run into the house scream-ing, "Is it here yet?" Three days later, my letter finally arrived. I carefully ripped the envelope to expose the inner treasure and basked in the joy of reading my two sentences. The process of communication by mail was a thrilling experience.

Today technology has changed every aspect of our lives, and is still changing it on a daily basis. The same letter sent via e-mail today would reach the recipient instantaneously and with no cost, less than the four cents of decades earlier.

Dentistry is no different than the rest of our society. Today, tech-nology has the changed the face of healthcare in multiple areas. From diagnosis through treatment, patients are cared for with efficiency, enhanced comfort, and improved outcomes.

In just the past few years, modern science has brought to the den-tal profession many advances. Some examples are digital cam-eras for both intra and extra oral use, computer based records, fiber optics to enhance vision during treatment, high speed halo-gen, plasma arc and LED lights to harden and strengthen the latest bonding materials – and the list goes on and on. Some-times technology not only gives us increased efficiency, but is healthier for the patient as well. In my opinion, the two areas in which technology in dentistry has excelled in both these aspects are computerized (digital) x-rays and lasers.

In 1895, Wilhelm Conrad Röntgen, a German Physicist, pro-duced and detected electromagnetic radiation in a wavelength range today known as X-rays or Röntgen rays, an achievement that earned him the first Nobel Prize in Physics in 1901. With this discovery was developed a new way of unfolding and re-vealing parts of the body that are hidden from plain sight. X-rays were put to diagnostic use very early, before the dangers of ion-izing radiation were discovered. Today, X-rays are the second most commonly used medical tests after blood tests. A dental X-ray image is formed by a controlled burst of radiation, which penetrates oral structures at different levels, depending on varying anatomical densities, before striking the film or digital sensor. Teeth appear lighter because less radiation penetrates them to reach the film. Cavities, infections and other changes in the bone density appear darker because X-rays readily penetrate these less dense structures. Dental restorations such as fillings and crowns may appear lighter or darker, depending on the density of the material that was used.

It is unfortunate that in the 21st century, most dental offices today are still taking X-rays with film, just like offices did decades ago. A film-based system has inherent flaws. It requires a fresh batch of film that needs to be shipped from a distributor with extra care taken during shipment to protect from radiation and heat. The film has to be processed in chemicals that are also governed by temperature and freshness. A special dark room has to be designated to develop the film. If any light leaks in during the processing the quality of the image will be compromised and may even be unusable. Film requires processing which on the average takes 6-8 minutes, and then has to be dried before being stored into the patient's file or sent elsewhere. If a new image has to be retaken, another 6-8 minutes are lost. The film size is only 1 inch by 1 ½ inches- so it is difficult to show patients what is going on in their mouths. Not to mention that of course, the processed film can be lost or misplaced. It is like mailing someone a letter when you need a response immediately.

Digital x-rays, on the other hand, save time. There is no processing; images are produced in seconds. No chemicals are needed, which reduces the cost and cuts down on environmental pollution. The sensor used is the same size as film, but the images are viewed on a large computer screen for patient education and explanation of treatment. With digital x-rays, the contrast can be changed to enhance proper reading of the x-ray even after exposure, while once film is processed it is unchangeable. However, the best advantage of all is that digital x-rays do not need the same amount of radiation exposure that film X-rays do, to ensure a proper diagnosis. This is because the digital sensor is more sensitive than film to lower doses of radiation. This reduces the radiation patients are exposed to by up to 90%! Modern technology wins hands down.

Once cavities are diagnosed, they need to be filled in order to prevent discomfort and infection. Patients want treatment done quickly and painlessly. Dentists have been searching for that holy grail of being efficient yet painless since the profession came into existence. Even dental advertisements from the early 20th century promoted painless dentistry. Today with dental lasers, we have come closer than ever before to that promise of a fast and comfortable dental experience.

LASER is an acronym for light amplification by stimulated emission of radiation. It is based on the theories developed by Albert Einstein in the early part of the twentieth century, but it was not until 1960 that Maiman introduced the first laser.

There are many different types of dental lasers, which are classified by their "active medium" – the part that determines their wavelength. Laser light has the ability to be absorbed, scattered, or reflected when it hits a target tissue. Absorption is the key of how laser light interacts with biological tissue. This absorption occurs either because of water, pigments, or other organic matter present in the tissue. Some are specific to certain parts of the mouth, and some can do almost all aspects of treatment from hard tissue (teeth and bone) to soft tissue (gums). This laser, which I consider a universal type of tool, is well absorbed by water and is able to mechanically ablate enamel, dentin, and bone. It also promotes healing and strengthens the body's own natural reparative processes.

Most people cringe at the sound of the drill, almost like fingernails scratching across a blackboard. The sound conjures up thoughts of discomfort from the heat, vibration, and pressure that can be associated with it.

Hocus-pocus, the universal dental laser enters the arena. This laser is a tremendous advancement and presents itself with no heat, vibration, or pressure generated. Most dental procedures can be performed with little or no need for anesthesia, a "no needles" technique resulting in fewer numb lips. The laser can be used in the treatment of gum disease and eliminates cutting with a scalpel and stitching the tissue afterwards. This laser can kill and desiccate the bacteria present in a dental pocket, reduce bleeding, swelling, and post-operative pain. And in most cases, only a topical anesthetic is needed.

Patients who have been hesitant about any form of periodontal treatment are amazed at the success, lack of postoperative pain, and the ability to resume their daily activities right after treatment.

One prime example is a woman who has been a patient of mine for over twenty years, who, when presented on her initial examination with diagnosis of moderate gum disease, refused all aspects of treatment other than fillings and cleanings. It was difficult to even get her to take routine x-rays! The position she took with her gum issues was that she would rather not know what was going on than be informed of her problems. She knew from reading about conventional periodontal surgery that it entailed cutting the gums with a scalpel, drilling the bone, and then stitching the gums up. She said to me on many occasions that she would rather lose all of her teeth than go through with the treatment. At her last appointment, we convinced her to get a full mouth of X-rays and took measurements of her bone levels. Her gum disease had advanced from moderate to bordering on severe. When this newer, advanced technological breakthrough was revealed to her, she was intrigued. When her treatment appointment came she was made comfortable with just a topical anesthetic, and was not only delighted that everything was accomplished in one sitting with no needles, but that she was able to go back to work the next day. These are the kind of successes in patient satisfaction that make this new approach rewarding not only for the patient, but also for the practitioner. At her two week postoperative visit, she reported no bleeding upon brushing, something she had experienced for years, and was absolutely amazed at the lack of any post-operative pain or sensitivity.

Another distinct advantage to these lasers is that they are precise when removing decay (cavities) on teeth. This conserves tooth structure and eliminates the possibilities of cracks and fractures due to vibrations caused by dental drills. Lasers can also enhance the ability to bond a stronger filling by altering the surface of the tooth. Elementary school children, as well as teenagers who have experienced the numb lip when having a tooth filled, are happy when fillings can be done in all regions of mouth quickly, because no anesthetic is necessary. They are also thrilled that there are absolutely no restrictions to how long you need to wait to eat after the laser is used, since there is no anesthetic that needs to wear off.

There are many points to consider when searching for that "right dentist." A dental office that is consistently updating its procedures to keep in pace with the latest research, an office in which the staff (dentists included!) continue their education constantly, and an office dedicated to the latest technology: That is an office which offers its patients the best.

About Dr. Herbert Schneider

Dr. Herbert Schneider has been in practice for over three decades and has made a distinctive mark upon his profession.

A member of many prestigious professional organizations, he has been the recipient of numerous awards over the years, including fellowship awards from the Academy of General Dentistry, the American Endodontic Society, and the World Clinical Laser Institute. He is also one of the few dentists awarded the prestigious Mastership award from the World Clinical Laser Institute.

His calm, yet precise manner, makes him a hit with his patients and he is equally as comfortable performing cosmetic makeovers on adults as he is relaxing and inviting to the youngest children.

Dr. Schneider feels that patients deserve the best treatment available. He has made his practice a model of the best that technology can offer. Technology, expertise, and caring are why Dr. Schneider feels proud to be a member of the dental profession.

CHAPTER 3

The Link Between Flossing, Diabetes, Inflammation, and Dentures

By Dr. Daniel Wolter

I was born near the end of the post-WWII "Baby Boom." At that time, my grandparents and most of their friends had pretty poor oral health. Back then, it was believed that losing most or all your teeth was the inevitable fate for nearly anyone who reached a certain age.

My grandmother was a perfect example of how things used to be. She lost all her teeth and wore complete dentures. She had several sets made, but was never comfortable with any of them. She never could chew efficiently, and couldn't smile or laugh confidently. I remember the "clicking" sound they would make whenever she was eating. My grandfather's situation was even worse, because he never was able to get a lower set that fit comfortably, so he always ate wearing only his uppers.

When I became a dentist, I made my grandmother a set of modern dentures which fit comfortably and allowed her to chew most foods. She was one of my first patients, and I spent many hours perfecting her dentures to the absolute best of my abilities. I can honestly tell you that helping my "Omi" regain her confidence, comfort, smile, and chewing ability was one of the most satisfying things I've ever done in my entire life, not just in my dental career. And, that annoying "clicking" was finally gone too, which was good for all of us.

She, like most others of her generation, lost her teeth due to gum disease (what dentists call "periodontitis"), a chronic, pain-free, destructive infection of the gums and jaw bones. It's hard to know now what other medical or systemic conditions may have contributed to her failing gums and eventual tooth loss. However, it's likely that inflammation and perhaps diabetes played an important role, as it has with millions of others over the years.

As a dentist, I diagnose and treat gum disease nearly every day. Unfortunately, it's still very common. In fact, next to the "common cold," it's the most widespread disease in the world. The American Dental Association estimates that it affects at least four out of five adults in the U.S. to some degree.

For centuries, periodontitis has been classified as a "degenerative" disease, meaning it was seen as an inevitable consequence of aging. It was only about 50 years ago that we discovered that bacterial "plaque" initiated gum disease, and persistent plaque caused its progression. So, gum disease is, in fact, a bacterial infection.

Everyone has a basic understanding of dental plaque: It's the yellowish substance which forms around teeth and gums over time. Initially, plaque is soft and easy to remove with a toothbrush and floss. If left undisturbed, however, it begins to mineralize and harden within about two days. At this stage, it's referred to as "calculus" or "tartar," and it can only be removed by a dental professional during a "cleaning."

If plaque and calculus are left in the mouth, they lead to significant oral health problems. However, they can cause all kinds of negative *systemic* consequences too, like diabetes. The connection between oral health and overall health, specifically diabetes, is due primarily to bacteria and their toxins from the mouth invading your bloodstream, and it can be summed up in one word: *Inflammation.*

The basic concept is simple: If you have plaque on your teeth, it slowly invades your gums and gets into the underlying structures. Over time, the invading bacteria and inflammation destroy the connective tissues and jaw bone around your teeth, causing them to loosen and eventually be lost. Moreover, bacteria and their toxins also "leak" into your blood vessels. From there, they can travel throughout your whole body. This constant and relentless invasion of micro-organisms puts a tremendous strain on your immune system and can cause all kinds of damage. In severe cases, unhealthy gums allow millions of bacteria to invade your body every single day, often for decades! Periodontal disease is especially destructive because it causes damage both by infection and inflammation.

Since we now know how gum disease develops, it's possible to prevent or interrupt that process. It doesn't generally matter how old you are, what your previous dental experiences have been, or what other dental problems you may have: If you don't have dental plaque, you won't get gum disease. So, it's very important to keep your teeth as clean as possible, and to get professional "cleanings" as often as possible, especially as you get older. In addition to plaque, there are a few risk factors which make it more likely for gum disease to develop. The most common of these seems to be *diabetes.*

Diabetes (the common name for *Diabetes mellitus*) refers to a group of metabolic disorders which affect the control of a person's blood sugar levels. In healthy individuals, the amount of sugar within the blood at any time is tightly regulated. In diabetics, however, blood sugar levels fluctuate and are often too high.

In adults, poor blood sugar control generally occurs when the pancreas doesn't produce enough insulin, a hormone which converts glucose (sugar) to glycogen (energy storage), thereby lowering and maintaining blood sugar levels within a narrow, healthy range.

Diabetes is a world-wide health crisis. Globally, there are over 285 million diabetics, and nearly 26 million in the U.S. That's over 11% of all adults. Alarmingly, more than one-fourth of U.S. adults with diabetes are not even aware they have the disease, and about two out of three diabetics are poorly controlled metabolically. Despite decades of research and progress, nearly two million new cases are still diagnosed each year. The financial cost of diabetes is also staggering. Direct medical costs plus indirect costs—such as missing work, disability, and premature death—total over $175 billion in the U.S. every single year.

Diabetes can have devastating and permanent effects on the body, some of which can be deadly. But, it can also have a major effect on your oral health, specifically the health of your gums. For example, diabetes makes you more susceptible to infections. And, guess what: Gum disease in an infection, as we learned earlier. So, having diabetes makes you more prone to developing gum disease. Furthermore, diabetes also makes infections more destructive, and treating them more difficult. To complicate things even more, diabetics don't heal well, so treating their gum disease is even more challenging. Because of these complications, it's common for diabetics to have periodontitis around every single tooth.

Interestingly, the association between diabetes and gum disease was first discussed by Hesi-Re, history's first dentist ever recorded, who lived in Egypt around 3,000 B.C. He noted a higher incidence of bleeding gums and tooth loss in his diabetic patients. However, only over the past decade or so have the underlying mechanisms been discovered. Perhaps more importantly, it has also become understood that this relationship is actually a "two-way street" – gum disease and diabetes are inter-related and can contribute to one another in both directions.

We all have experience with inflammation, the natural reaction of your body to an irritant or toxin. For example, if you get a splinter stuck under your skin, the area around it becomes tender, swollen, warm, and red. These are typical signs of your body responding to an invasion by a foreign substance. Similarly, when your bloodstream has bacteria circulating through it, your body reacts with inflammation. However, when inflammation is on the "inside," you usually don't see or feel it, but it still causes lots of damage.

Today, we can quantify inflammation with a simple blood test that measures C-Reactive Protein (CRP). This "inflammatory marker" is an indicator of the overall level of inflammation within your body. It's not a specific test for periodontitis, but it gives insight into how stressed and active your immune system is. In people with untreated gum disease, CRP levels can soar dramatically, sometimes more than ten times the normal amount.

Having a persistent, low-grade infection in your mouth (periodontitis) also *directly* stimulates your body to release more glucose (sugar) into your bloodstream. When cells are defending themselves against bacteria and inflammation, they use more glucose for energy, so your body gives them what they need. This effect is especially harmful for diabetics, who have difficulty controlling their blood sugar levels. The last thing they need is for their unhealthy gums to constantly trigger the release of more glucose.

The study and treatment of gum disease and its effects throughout the body is known as "periodontal medicine." Unfortunately, this field is still fairly new, and we don't have all the answers yet. However, we do understand the relationship between dental plaque and diabetes quite well. There are several proposed ways diabetes can develop in adults. Over a thousand scientific studies have proposed that inflammation within the body directly contributes to—and actually causes—diabetes. Since systemic inflammation, for millions of people, is caused *directly* by untreated gum disease, that link is now also clear.

So, uncontrolled dental plaque and increased inflammation

throughout the body are not just risk factors for diabetes. They're not just complicating factors. Today, we can confidently say that untreated gum disease can actually *cause* diabetes, and that controlling or eliminating gum disease can improve the course of diabetes. That's a pretty powerful statement. In fact, having ongoing gum disease can increase your risk of developing diabetes by a staggering 300%! Stated another way, periodontal disease can increase your risk of developing diabetes to over 90%.

This understanding has radically changed how dentists approach gum disease and its treatment. These insights have also affected how many physicians examine and diagnose their diabetic patients. Periodontitis is no longer accepted as an inevitable consequence of getting older. It's no longer seen as a localized problem affecting only teeth and oral health. It's no longer of interest only to dentists and hygienists.

One of my primary missions as a dentist is to make my patients, physicians, and the public more aware of this widespread problem, and to offer modern solutions which make sense and are predictable. Today, gum disease is known to be *deadly* if left untreated and allowed to progress! It must be addressed early, continuously, and assertively, and these insights should be shared with everyone in the healthcare field.

Your responsibility is to let your dentist know about your general health, and your physician should know if you have gum disease, especially if you already have diabetes, or you're having difficulty with blood sugar control. Fortunately, more and more physicians are working together with dentists to diagnose and treat these two inter-related conditions, and modern treatment options offer more hope than ever before. When everyone works together, it's common today to help treat diabetes with dental gum therapy, and to help treat gum disease with tighter diabetic control. So, don't be surprised if your dentist orders a blood test to check for diabetes or general inflammation, or your physician looks into your mouth and checks for swollen, bleeding gums in the future.

Furthermore, it's important for diabetics to see their dentist right away if they notice any of the following problems: gums which are swollen, gums which bleed when brushing or flossing, gums which are pulling away from the teeth, persistent bad breath or a bad taste, teeth which are loose or moving, any change in the bite, any change in the fit of an oral appliance, or yellowish fluid (pus) around the gums.

It's also important for your dentist to know if you have been diagnosed with diabetes, so its oral effects can be minimized. The most important information to share is: When you were diagnosed, how well controlled it is, any other recent changes in your medical history, and the names of all the medications you're taking.

The most accurate way to determine diabetic control is with the blood test known as "Hemoglobin-A1C" (HbA1C or A1C). This test gives an indication of how high or low your blood sugar levels have been, on average, over the past two to three months. Because it's an average over time, it's a more accurate indicator of overall diabetic control, and not as sensitive to fluctuations, like daily blood sugar measurements.

In the early stages of gum disease, dental treatments are quick, easy, affordable, and nearly 100% effective. If gum disease is allowed to progress, however, treatments become much more difficult, costly, and less effective. In advanced cases, even with all of today's advances and modern techniques, tooth removal can sometimes be the only remaining option. So, if you think your gums may not be as healthy as they should be, get help right away. Gum disease *always* gets worse if left untreated.

While we still don't have a true "cure" for periodontitis (since new bacteria are always entering the mouth and forming new plaque colonies…it's a never-ending battle to stop this process), we have developed treatment modalities which can offer predictable, stable, long-term successes. "Deep cleanings," lasers, antiseptics, and antibiotics have largely replaced the invasive surgeries of the past, and these treatments have become more comfortable and widely accepted by the public.

Most of us recognize that lifestyle choices, diet, exercise, and habits have a huge influence on what will happen with our health in the future. Included in the list of things you should be doing to promote a healthy life are brushing and flossing every single day, visiting your dentist regularly, and investing the time and money needed to keep your mouth as healthy as possible. By the way, if you don't like flossing, or find it inconvenient, you should know that dedicated flossers, on average, live four years longer than non-flossers! That's a powerful reminder of how important it is to keep your mouth healthy and limit your body's overall inflammation. Remember, if your mouth isn't healthy, you're not healthy.

For some, maintaining great oral health takes only a simple and small investment. For many others, it requires a significant change in priorities and attitude. However, it should be obvious now that a healthy mouth will not just increase your appearance, self-esteem, and ability to smile and eat (as we've always known), but will also reduce your body's inflammation, reduce your risk of developing diabetes and other life-threatening illnesses, reduce some of the difficulty controlling your blood sugar levels if you already have diabetes, and potentially add extra years and quality to your life. Healthy gums really can give you a better and longer life.

A strong commitment to preventive oral healthcare, including professional dental check-ups, x-rays, and cleanings, is extremely important for all adults, but even more for diabetics. Here's the bottom line: if you make excellent oral health a priority right now, you will improve your overall health and your life. It's really that simple. If you get your gum disease treated right now, you'll likely live longer, and get to spend more quality time with your children, friends, and loved ones. If you get serious about a healthy mouth, you'll be on a path to feeling and looking better.

And, vice versa, if you control your diabetes more tightly, you'll have a healthier mouth.

The easiest way for diabetics to maintain their oral health is with excellent oral hygiene practices at home—brushing at least twice daily and flossing every day—and more frequent dental evaluations and preventive procedures. Waiting six months between dental visits is rarely advisable for adult diabetics. Just as importantly, blood glucose levels should be controlled as tightly as possible.

If you maintain meticulous control over your diabetes, and choose a dental team experienced in periodontal medicine and treating diabetics, you'll be able to keep your gums and teeth healthy and beautiful for life, regardless of any additional risks or challenges diabetes may bring. Better yet, if you keep your gums healthy from the beginning, you may never develop diabetes at all.

About Dr. Daniel Wolter

Dr. Daniel Wolter grew-up as an "Army Brat," and spent most of his young life overseas. His family was stationed in Munich, Germany during his high school years. After graduation, he decided to stay in Germany to attend the University of Munich, where he completed his dental studies in 1991.

Transitioning from the American educational system to studying at a post-graduate level in the German university system proved to be quite a challenge. However, it also led to the development of a unique, complex, and complimentary perspective about dentistry and oral health, which was distinctive from what his U.S. counterparts were being taught at that time.

Many of the advantages of this perspective were formed through learning about dentistry as a sub-specialty of medicine, integrated holistically as a definitive part of overall health. While the mouth and teeth have distinct problems and conditions which dentists routinely treat, they should not be viewed as separate from the rest of the body or human experience.

After graduating from dental school, he practiced in Munich for a few years while also pursuing an additional doctorate at the University of Mainz, which he achieved "with honors" in 1995.

Soon after that, he moved to Chicago to earn an additional two-year post-doctoral Masters Degree in "Advanced General Dentistry," while also being named Assistant Professor of Clinical Dentistry at Northwestern University Dental School.

He is very proud that fewer than 1% of dentists have attained his level of advanced education and academic distinction. His unique background and perspective, experience in research and teaching, and over 21 years of "hands-on" clinical expertise allow him to provide the most contemporary, up-to-date dental solutions available today.

Dr. Wolter left Chicago in 2006 to enjoy the sunny skies and friendly folks of Arizona. His Goodyear, AZ practice, *Millennium Dental Arts*, cares primarily for Baby Boomers and Seniors, with a focus on complex restorative dental care, esthetic dentistry, dental implants, and periodontal medicine.

As the concept of "mouth-body health" becomes more widely understood, the connection and interplay between oral health and systemic health becomes more clear, and the public becomes more and more interested in wellness and longevity, his practice continues to evolve from providing world-class "tooth" care to modern-day "oral, dental, and systemic health" care.

To learn more about Dr. Wolter, his amazing team, and what modern dentistry can do for you, please visit: www.MDA-Dentist.com, or call 623-536-6789.

CHAPTER 4

Benefits of Orthodontic Treatments

By Daniel L.W. Fishel, DMD

It is widely accepted that orthodontic treatment has significant self-esteem benefits for the children and adults who receive treatment. In addition, much has been written regarding the benefits of straight teeth on oral hygiene and the ability to better keep one's teeth clean. The aforementioned benefits, I would argue, are the primary reasons parents pursue orthodontic treatment for their children and adults seek orthodontic treatment for themselves later in life.

It is wonderful for our patients that, today, we have technologies that very efficiently and quickly provide straight, easily cleansable teeth. Starting with the diagnosis, we have the ability to scan the mouth with an intraoral camera, providing digital, computer-generated models without the need for impressions. Radiography has also greatly improved, with the ability to digitally obtain x-rays within seconds without the need for expensive processing rooms, equipment and chemicals. In addition, three-dimensional radiographs allow for the imaging of craniofacial structures and relationships that were previously unattainable. Upon the orthodontist determining a treatment plan for the patient, indirect bonding trays can be fabricated, allowing for ideal placement of braces on all teeth within minutes; historically, braces were individually placed on teeth via an "eyeballing" technique, introducing potential error into bracket placement and, therefore, precise tooth movement. The newest generations of brackets are now fabricated to be self-ligating, negating the need for elastic or stainless steel ties to hold the wire in the bracket, improving oral hygiene, decreasing previously bulky bracket profiles and greatly decreasing friction, therefore, speeding up tooth movement. Lastly, the orthodontic wires used in the early and middle stages of a typical treatment are super-elastic, lighter in force application to the teeth and long-lasting in nature, meaning tooth movement is less painful and significant tooth movement can be performed without the need for monthly orthodontic appointments.

It is an exciting time to be an orthodontist! Demand for treatment is driven largely by our desire to provide the best for our children, and technology has simplified providing exceptional results…WHEN APPLIED PROPERLY!

The purpose of this chapter is to provide the reader with a very honest and blunt assessment of orthodontics as it exists today. At times, this assessment may even sound cynical. It is the hope, however, that those who seek orthodontic treatment for their children or for themselves will be better educated by this chapter, allowing for better consumption of orthodontic services.

IT'S NOT ABOUT STRAIGHTENING TEETH!

This chapter began with commentary regarding our desire to obtain gorgeous smiles for our children and ourselves. Improved self-esteem, an improved social life and the ability to attain a better job, and therefore lifestyle, are all cited as reasons to have a great smile. Would it surprise you, then, that months and months of braces-wear are actually a very small part of long-term stability and alignment of teeth?

I believe that braces are a relatively insignificant part of orthodontic treatment. The most significant step in a patient's orthodontic treatment actually occurs before any orthodontic appliances are used: making the diagnosis. The orthodontist MUST determine why teeth are misaligned. I tell my patients that teeth are not genetically programmed to erupt in a misaligned fashion; teeth have one goal, and that goal is to erupt. If given adequate space, teeth will largely erupt into proper position and in a very acceptable alignment without issue. The problem, however, is many individuals, today, lack adequate spacing for eruption of all permanent teeth, and, therefore, teeth rotate, angulate and squeeze any which way they can to erupt...and it oftentimes doesn't look pretty.

Orthodontists don't just straighten teeth...or, at least, they shouldn't just straighten teeth. As a profession, our goal should be to provide a foundation for teeth to function properly and to be appropriately positioned for smile and facial esthetics. Quite simply, this foundation is the jawbones. The jawbones consist of alveolar bones, which are the upper and lower horseshoe-shaped bones that teeth are positioned in, and basal bones, which are the underlying bones supporting alveolar bones. Basal bones give us our outward appearance, such as cheek and chin prominence/form. Due to the fact that they support alveolar bone, they also largely determine how teeth are positioned, whether it be by nature or by the orthodontist. So, if basal bones are not appropriately formed or positioned, we cannot expect to provide a perfectly functioning or esthetic smile.

The single most important treatment I provide for my patients on a daily basis is growth modification. We are, of course, three-dimensional beings, and I, therefore, must assess basal bone growth in three dimensions to determine my ability to straighten teeth and provide appropriate function and smile esthetics. There are many ways jawbones can be malformed, all of which have detrimental effects on my ability to provide an ideal orthodontic result.

In my practice, the two most common jaw malformations I see are:

1). an upper jaw that is too small in width; and

2). a lower jaw that is too small in depth (i.e., the chin sets back relative to the rest of the face).

We explain to parents and adult patients that, in order to provide an ideal orthodontic result, we must start by fixing the underlying bones (i.e., provide a good foundation). This can be done in two ways: 1) functional or growth modification appliances, which take advantage of bone pliability and growth potential, to adequately size and position bones; or 2) surgical repositioning of bones into a position that allows for orthodontic success. As you can imagine, parents and patients are much more amenable to the first option.

Luckily, when a child is first seen in my office by approximately age 10, the single most common growth problem I see, a narrow upper jaw, can be addressed non-surgically with an appliance called a rapid palatal expander. The appliance is fixed, or glued, to the palatal aspect of the upper teeth, and an expansion key is used in the home to gradually widen the upper jaw over the course of one to three weeks, on average. My goal is to widen the upper jaw so that it is appropriately sized to match the width of the lower jaw, allowing for appropriate positioning and relationship of the upper and lower teeth to each other. Parents, however, notice that their child's smile looks wide and gorgeous, and very rarely do we need to remove teeth to achieve tooth alignment. I cannot recall a time when parents have told me that they didn't like the look of a wider upper jaw and smile for their child; it is a win-win situation for all involved.

A majority of other jawbone growth issues are difficult to treat non-surgically, at least in my experience. For patients who, for example, have a significant deficiency in the front-to-back growth of the lower jaw and chin, I recommend surgical treatment (specifically, advancement) of the lower jaw. We make it very clear to parents and patients that, if an ideal orthodontic result is desired, surgical treatment must be pursued. We do not, however, pressure patients to pursue surgical treatment; surgical orthodontic treatment is a very serious, time consuming and costly venture. It must be well thought out by all involved, and the benefits must be weighed against the downsides of the treatment. At very least, if a parent or patient has any desire for a perfect orthodontic result, we recommend that they see an oral surgeon, who would perform the surgery, to gain as much information as possible to make an informed decision on the potential surgical treatment being pursued.

WHO CARES IF IT'S NOT PERFECT

I have many parents and patients that say they don't care if their teeth or their child's teeth are perfect…just make them as good as they can be. I can appreciate that. I have three children, and at least one of them will have a lower jaw deficiency that will benefit from surgery to produce an ideal orthodontic result. My wife (who is also a dentist) and I are not sure if we want to put our daughter through surgery to make her 'perfect.' I must make one thing clear, though: my wife and I are educated with regards to this decision, and upon weighing our options and potential results, costs and complications, the risk-to-reward ratio may not be in our daughter's favor. I, however, should not be the person making the ultimate decision for my patients. I feel it very important to present ALL information and treatment options I am aware of regarding a particular problem and let parents and patients decide upon the treatment that will best serve them and their specific situation. It is my hope that consumers of orthodontic services see those in the orthodontic community as educators, providing valuable information with which the consumer can make appropriate decisions.

Specifically, I not only educate parents and patients on the esthetics of a perfect smile, but also the potential long-term dental, periodontal (gum) and temporomandibular joint consequences of a less-than-perfect bite. I have the very unique luxury of being both an orthodontist and a periodontist (gum surgeon). I, therefore, literally and figuratively see the smiles on the faces of the children for whom I complete orthodontic treatment, as well as the frustration on the faces of the adults who need periodontal treatment due to alveolar bone loss and receding gums. I feel very strongly that providing an ideally functioning bite significantly reduces a patient's future risk of caries (cavities), tooth breakage, periodontal disease and orthodontic relapse (teeth becoming misaligned). I explain to parents and patients that the human mouth is simply a complex machine. When all of the pieces function well together, the machine lasts longer with less needed maintenance. Conversely, when the pieces are haphazardly forced to function together, undue wear and breakdown occurs.

A proper occlusion (bite) is one in which both the right and left temporomandibular joints function properly and all teeth function together in such a manner to provide for mastication (chewing) and speech, while protecting each other from accelerated wear, breakdown and/or loss. Back teeth and the immediately surrounding jawbone are anatomically designed to take purely vertical forces for crushing food and protecting the smaller rooted front teeth from excessive forces during chewing. Front teeth are designed to incise and glide against each other in a nonvertical fashion, taking these stresses away from the back teeth. So, as you can see, all teeth must be properly positioned for the benefit of the whole functioning system. When the function of the temporomandibular joints or the position and function of the teeth is compromised, a myriad of complications can arise, including joint clicking and/or pain, muscle tightness and/or pain, tooth breakage, periodontal bone loss, caries and/or inability to chew and speak properly.

Frustratingly, complications associated with a poorly functioning bite may take years, or even decades, to manifest, and rarely do these complications occur simultaneously. For that reason, we lose the forest for the trees and simply address the problem at hand, such as need for a single composite restoration, crown or periodontal treatment. If an astute dentist determines that the patient's bite is the primary cause of his/her dental disease, such significant orthodontic and surgical treatment is often needed to reverse course, that patients become overwhelmed by treatment scope, length and cost. Patients are often, therefore, doomed to a life of patchwork dentistry in which the ultimate hope is that their teeth outlive them.

I am especially sensitive to the above scenario due to fact that nearly 100% of the periodontal patients I treat suffer from a significant malocclusion (bad bite). The periodontal profession largely attributes periodontal bone loss to the human body's reaction to bacteria, and it is indisputable that there are differing species of bacteria in these patients relative to periodontally healthy patients; but I feel that we fail to appreciate the extent to which the bite can influence one's periodontal health. Afflicted patients have been told for decades that they have been negligent in appropriate oral hygiene…that they don't brush and floss adequately. Those with receding gums and loss of bone on the outer surfaces of their teeth have been told that they brush too hard… that they should use a softer toothbrush. One patient is negligent and the next is overly diligent…but what they share is that both suffer from periodontal bone loss.

Could there be a different explanation as to why periodontal bone loss occurs, or at least an additional primary cause for this affliction? I would argue that multiple factors must be present in order for an individual to suffer from periodontal disease, but consistently the lack of a properly functioning bite is what I see in my specialty practice. Yes, inadequate home care, smoking, uncontrolled diabetes and stress are found with many of these patients, but the common thread is consistently a pathologic bite.

In discussing my findings with these patients and giving treatment options, most are somewhat overwhelmed, some depressed and some upset. Almost all, however, are quick to agree that their problems are not simply negligence. Due to financial and time constraints, we are oftentimes left with pursuing traditional solutions to address these problems, such as deep scalings and periodontal surgery, with the patient's understanding that these solutions are simply a patch, prolonging the life of the teeth but not truly addressing or eliminating all of the causes of the problem.

MINIMIZING YOUR OR YOUR CHILD'S FUTURE ORAL HEALTH RISK

If these treatments are not within your budget or time limitations, at least question a dental professional regarding the benefits of an occlusal guard (also called a night guard or occlusal splint). When I have a patient who cannot afford complex orthodontic treatment, or I have a patient who underwent orthodontic treatment but was not willing to undergo surgical treatment to idealize the bite, I recommend an occlusal guard. An occlusal guard is a clear acrylic or plastic appliance that snaps onto the upper or lower teeth, providing an artificial, ideal bite. For patients who have undergone orthodontic treatment, an occlusal guard also serves as a retainer. These appliances, in my opinion, greatly reduce dental problems when they are adjusted and used properly. A dentist must fabricate and adjust the occlusal guard, and follow-up should be performed at regular intervals to assure that the appliance continues to function properly, taking maximal stresses off of the dentition, periodontium and temporomandibular joints.

BE AN EDUCATED CONSUMER OF DENTAL CARE

As we conclude this chapter, you may be having the same overwhelming feelings many of my patient's express following a consult in my office. You may even be able to identify with the scenarios outlined above. Please, use the information in this chapter to be a better consumer of dental services. Question your dentist or dental specialist on the treatments available to provide an ideal bite. Although initially overwhelming, the benefits resulting from addressing these issues promptly will undoubtedly reduce the scope and cost of your or your child's dental treatment in the future.

About Dr. Daniel Fishel

Daniel L.W. Fishel, DMD, is one of approximately twenty individuals in the United States dual-trained in the dental specialties of orthodontics and periodontics.

Dr. Fishel practices in multiple locations in south central Pennsylvania, including Harrisburg, York and Hanover. He emphasizes educating his patients on the best treatments dentistry has to offer – providing orthodontic, periodontal and dental implant treatments that maximize dental health and longevity, as well as quality of life.

CHAPTER 5

ALTERNATIVE THERAPIES FOR MIGRAINE
Or...Migraine Is A Disease Of Dental Origin

By Michael Steinberg, DDS

When I graduated New York University College of Dentistry in 1987, I could not have imagined that in August of 2001, the course of my life and of my career would be so profoundly changed. That was when I began providing and using a DENTAL DEVICE that had recently been cleared by the Food and Drug Administration (FDA) for the Treatment and PREVENTION of MIGRAINE HEADACHE. That's right! Me! A DENTIST! I was beginning to treat a disease and a malady that had plagued me for much of my life. I waded into a pool where only neurologists swam with authority. A pool where lowly tradespersons like dentists, chiropractors, acupuncturists, and therapists of the physical or the mental variety would, at best, be soundly ridiculed. At worst, they would be swallowed alive like so many herring in a sea of killer whales. How did I come by this audacity and arrogance? How did I come to the point where I would feel confident that the patients I would treat for migraine and tension headaches had at least as good, and maybe even a better chance of becoming pain free greatly improving their quality of life, than if they followed the path of traditional physicians with their pharmaceutical remedies?

HEADACHES ARE A DRAG!

For as long as I could remember, I had headaches. If I wasn't having one, I was waiting and worrying about the next one. As a kid, it was never severe enough to warrant a doctor's visit. An over the counter remedy like Tylenol (acetaminophen), or aspirin, or that new thing called Motrin (ibuprofen) was usually enough to stop those chronic daily headaches from blossoming into a full blown migraine. Usually, I would awaken with some degree of discomfort, take some OTC's (non-prescription, Over the Counter medications such as Tylenol or Advil) and go about my day. We now measure the level of pain on a scale of zero through ten. A zero means there is no pain and the patient feels great. A ten means the worst level of pain imaginable. A person with a level 10 is incapacitated. Even on a day when I woke up with only a 2 or 3, I still took some OTC's so as not to worry that the pain might increase. This went on throughout much of high school, college and dental school. What seemed ironic to me was how often my headaches got worse at those times when I should have been carefree and relaxed. It happened on weekends, on holidays, after the final exams, after the term projects, and so on. As I will explain later, I was not the only one with this pattern of suffering. It robs many victims, especially celebrities, of their ability to wind down, to relax and to heal. Turning to alcohol or to sedatives of the prescribed or illegal varieties, it is not surprising how often these unhealthy habits and behaviors lead to addiction, to disease, and to death.

After marrying my wonderful wife just before my senior year, and after four years of rigorous training at NYU Dental College, I was accepted into a residency in general dentistry at Metropolitan Hospital Center on the upper West Side of Manhattan. NOW I was going to relax! The uncertainties of passing all my courses and clinics in school were gone. All the risk was gone. I had my license to practice dentistry and was hired to do just that while gaining experience and still being able to ask for a second opinion if needed. I even got paid the princely sum of $27,000 for that year of learning. I was on cruise control, right? WRONG! My headaches got worse. Being in a hospital setting, I figured "why not get a CAT scan and see if anything shows up? When the scan was over, I was barely out of that noisy machine when a Pakistani resident said to me "We think you have a pituitary adenoma. It's a tiny TUMOR at the base of the brain but don't worry. We can easily get to it by cutting through the mouth, over the teeth and below the nose. Can we put you on the schedule for FRIDAY? "I don't think so!" I said. After having my neurologist cousin look at the scan, I had an MRI of my head and nothing (of medical interest) was found in there. I came *THISCLOSE* to having an invasive, potentially life threatening and UNNECESSARY medical procedure! Later on, I learned a technique of meditation that seemed to be useful. That's when an MD friend of mine introduced me to a drug called Fioricet. By the time a very upset stomach made me quit the Fioricet, I had forgotten how to meditate. I was back to square one.

EVERYTHING, EVEN A BAD BACK, HAPPENS FOR A REASON

One day in April 2001, I received in my office a medium-sized package from Dr. Jim Boyd, a dentist in San Diego. Inside, I found a very complete sample kit for making the dental appliance called the NTI-TSS. NTI-TSS stands for Nociceptive Trigeminal Inhibition – Tension Suppression System. In short, it lowers the tension in your head by inhibiting and lowering the pain signals coming from the trigeminal nerve that comes from the brain. (And THAT'S why we just say "NTI"). A very complete PowerPoint DVD with dazzling illustrations was also included. It said on it "APPROVED BY THE FDA to TREAT TEMPOROMANDIBULAR DISORDERS" I thought "YUK! *Nobod*y likes or wants to treat TMJ! That's VOODOOLAND!

The only TMJ lecture I had seen, through eyes glazed-over, until then (and even THAT I went to by accident) taught me that TMJ is a problem that afflicts mostly crazy *women* and that only a witch doctor, or maybe the man who gave the lecture can even HOPE to treat them!" And so, that very generous gift of NTI samples sat on the shelf. In June, when the *husband* of one of my favorite patients mentioned at his visit that he had sore jaw joints, I figured "why not?" And so, I made my first NTI. It really helped! In July of 2001, my wife and my daughter were going to spend some nights in a bungalow in the Hamptons. The sound my daughter made at night when grinding her teeth resembled that of crashing dishes in a restaurant kitchen. I had to do something to rescue my wife from that. My daughter, 10 1/2 years old at the time, actually wore the thing and the nights passed quietly. I was two for two! In late July, I suffered back spasms one day, stayed home from work, and saw a news story on the noontime newscast that I would otherwise not have seen. "Next up after the break, How Your Dentist Can Heal Your MIGRAINE Headaches." When it came on TV, I jumped up and cried (because my back hurt), "That's It! That's the NTI!" I just HAD to learn more.

My family and I flew to San Diego for 1 day of lecture and 3 days of vacation. As if to get in the mood, I had a major migraine event on the plane. In the morning, Dr. Boyd lectured. In the afternoon, Dr. Boyd asked, as I knew he would, for a volunteer. Well, the last time I jumped up that fast was in fifth grade when the teacher asked if someone would carry home a science project for the prettiest girl in the class! This time, however, I was NOT mortally embarrassed.

All I can say now is that since that day, the control that migraine over me is very, very small. I may still get one if some other causes of migraine occur. For me, it could be a result of becoming dehydrated, or from insufficient sleep. If I get lazy and fail to wear my NTI's to sleep (yes. For me, I need a lower AND an upper NTI), the headaches can start to worm their way back into the picture.

TYPES OF HEADACHE – BRIEF DESCRIPTIONS FROM THE CONVENTIONAL MEDICINE PLAYBOOK

1). <u>The Weekend or the "Let-Down" headache</u> - As I described earlier, the stressful situation is behind you. Unless you have a reliable technique for relaxation, all that energy that you focused on your issue doesn't automatically go away just because you're finished. In May of 2005, On CNN, Larry King had a panel discussion on headache. One guest was Susan Olsen who played Cindy on the TV show "The Brady Bunch." From Monday thru Thursday they recorded the show. After the shoot, while the rest of the cast went to a party, Ms. Olsen would go home, suffering a migraine. Every Time. I have patients who are school teachers who tell me that right after class ends, on the way home, they have to pop in their NTI so the pent-up stress of the day doesn't start a migraine.

2). <u>Tension-Type</u> - Usually feels like a hat band is being tightened around the head. It can last 30 minutes to several hours. Exercise usually IMPROVES symptoms of this mild to moderate pain. It sometimes morphs into a migraine. OTC pain relievers usually help tension type headaches.

3). <u>The Migraine</u> - Often a one-sided headache, migraine can be a disabling event. If you want to understand how severe it can be, go look at migraine art at the website of the AmericanHeadacheSociety.org. There you will find pictures drawn by children whose vocabulary cannot adequately describe their pain. It may be accompanied by visual disturbances, nausea, sensitivity to light and sound. Movement will make it worse. The advent of the TRIPTAN class of drugs has been a true game changer. Often very effective, they are the biggest tool in the arsenal of conventional medicine. They do have side effects, and cannot be used by airline pilots on duty, or by pregnant women. Overuse of these and other drugs can lead to......

4). <u>Medication Overuse or Rebound Headaches</u> - If you take medications for headaches more than 10 times per month, you are at greater risk for this type. Gradual withdrawal of pain drugs is the preferred treatment here.

5). <u>Cluster headache</u> - Also known as the "suicide" headache, this one features severe to excruciating pain. There maybe a runny nose, tearing and a droopy eyelid on the affected side. It can occur several times a day and last from 15 minutes to 3 hours. Inhaled oxygen is the preferred treatment.

WHAT IS THE NTI –TSS AND HOW DOES IT WORK?

As recently as this month, major magazines and journals consistently leave the NTI-TSS out of their "Latest Developments in Migraine Treatment" themed articles. This disservice to their readers continues in spite of these facts:

- In July of 2001, the NTI-TSS was cleared by the FDA for the treatment and prevention of Migraine.

- In the 8-week study that earned the FDA clearance, there were no side effects and no new pain.

- 82% of NTI users had an average of 77% reduction in migraine events.

- Medication use was reduced by almost 50%.

- Nausea was reduced by 78%.

- Light sensitivity was reduced by 66%.

- Sound sensitivity was reduced by 68%.

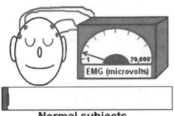
Normal subjects

Chronic Headache Patients

One thing that is observed in nearly all migraine sufferers is tenderness around the head. Medical studies confirm that people who suffer from migraine clench their teeth at night. This causes significant contraction of the muscles on the side of the head. There's no known way to stop this clenching and some medications may even make it worse. Most clenchers are UNAWARE of their clenching. The nerves that run to and from these muscles transmit irritating signals to the part of the brain that is supposed to manage and modulate pain signals. This region, called the *Trigeminal Nucleus Caudalis* enters a state of hypersensitivity. Now, it fails to filter and modify all the incoming noxious and irritating pain signals. In this state of allodynia, things that normally don't hurt or irritate now do so. Just as a gentle stroking of sunburned skin brings great pain, things such as sounds, light or movement can disable someone experiencing a migraine attack.

There are several possible contributors to migraines. Picture, if you will, a big bucket. Above it are five faucets of different sizes with different color fluids flowing into the bucket. One faucet represents clenching. Another could be hormone changes. Another is stress, etc. This picture tells us why the chiropractor can shut off one faucet and take credit for the cure. Or the drugs shut off a faucet. When the bucket overflows, a migraine is in progress, and we cannot tell which faucet is most responsible – it's all mingled together. (There is also a small hole in the bottom to let some of the troubled waters flow out.) **Our theory is that the clenching is the biggest faucet. For NTI dentists, it is also by far the easiest to shut off.**

The NTI-TSS is a dental appliance that when worn, reduces the intensity of nighttime jaw clenching by over 77%.

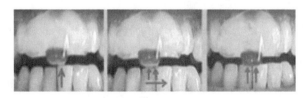

Whether it is worn on the upper jaw or the lower, our goal is to have it contact ONLY the incisor teeth of the opposite arch. This causes the muscles that close the jaw to contract with a much lower intensity. This aspect is very useful to people who exercise with weights. It also protects the teeth and the dental restorations. You can demonstrate this for yourself. Put your hands on the side of your head above the temples and clench down. Feel the muscles bulge? Now put a hard object like a toothbrush handle or a pencil between your front teeth. Clench again. The closing muscles cannot muster the same intensity of closing. Now the muscles can get more rest. The jaw joints can also get nourishment from the joint fluids if they're not being squeezed dry like a sponge for hours at a time.

The results I've seen over the last 11 years have made providing relief from headaches the most gratifying part of my practice.

There is much more information available at my website (www. yourfavoritedentist.com) as well as the sites posted at the end of this chapter. There are several other alternatives to conventional medical medication therapy. Some of these include BOTOX, Nutritional Supplements, Over-The-Counter medications like MIGRALEX (a combination of aspirin and Magnesium).

Since stress is by far the most prevalent of the triggers of migraine, stress reduction techniques such as Meditation, Yoga, Physical therapy, hypnosis, and Meridian Tapping can be most helpful.

Whatever you try, if it fails to work for you, please, don't ever give up. Keep trying new and even strange things like going to the dentist. One of my most precious mentors, Dr. Barry Glassman of Allentown, PA tells a story of a woman who suffered migraines for decades. After trying all of the treatments in his arsenal, he told her he had no other choices and she would have to try something else but he didn't know what. After six months and reading her 23rd book on migraine, she looked to see if she had any food allergies. It turned out that migraine was her only symptom of her allergy to WHEAT!

Never give up. But try a dentist if you haven't done so yet.

Links: www.headachehope.com
        www.theheadachecenter.com
        www.headaches.org
        www.americanheadachesociety.com

About Dr. Michael Steinberg

Michael Steinberg, DDS - also known as Your Favorite Dentist - is a dentist practicing in Brooklyn, New York since 1990. A graduate of New York University College of Dentistry, he completed a residency in general dentistry at Metropolitan Hospital Center in Manhattan, New York. Dr. Steinberg has received extensive training in Painful Disorders of the Head & Neck, as well as in Sleep Disorders and Dental Sleep medicine.

Dr. Michael Steinberg has authored articles on Dental Treatment of Migraine Headache, Nutritional Support for Periodontal Disease, on Snoring and Sleep Apnea, and on the connection between Oral Disease and Overall Wellness. These articles have appeared in publications such as Bottom Line Natural Healing, The Journal of the New York State Academy of General Dentistry and Clinician's Advisor. He has also lectured on these topics and continues to do so.

Dr. Steinberg's passion is to find and to provide for the dental health, and thereby the overall health, of his patients and his community, using therapeutic modalities that remain underdeveloped in the settings of traditional healthcare.

His most cherished claim to fame is that of being the husband of Miriam Steinberg for 25 years, and of being the father of daughter Adina, and son Benjamin.

He is a member of the following societies:
• American Dental Association
• Academy of General Dentistry
• American Academy of Dental Sleep Medicine
• American Academy of Craniofacial Pain

To learn more about Dr. Steinberg, go to his website at:
www.yourfavoritedentist.com

CHAPTER 6

Managing Expectations is Critical in Orthodontic Treatment

By Dr. Hisham Kaloti

On a storming late afternoon in March, a mom and her son walked into my office signed their names on the sign-in sheet and sat quietly in the corner, trying to shake off their soaking wet coats. It was already getting dark out, so earlier, when we received a cancellation notice from the last patient of the day, we thought we may be headed home early for a change... however, that day, we weren't that lucky. The mom seemed visibly agitated, but the son didn't seemed too bothered being in a dental office. She was sitting at the edge of her seat, clenching her son's backpack and a large manila envelope over her lap as if hugging it tightly. My assistant, Jean, proceeded to welcome them, introduce herself and escort them promptly back to the dental operatory like she would for any other patient. She quizzed them about the nature of their visit today, the boy's medical history, allergies...etc, but as soon as Jean started asking about the boy's dental history, the mom paused, abruptly stood up, and asked to speak with the doctor in private. It wasn't unusual for moms to be protective about their children's medical information, so Jean didn't give it much thought as she ushered her into the private consult room to await my arrival. A few minutes later, I walked

65

into the consult room, introduced myself to the mom, as she still clung to a rather large manilla envelope...

"I understand you requested to speak with me, how can I help?" I asked, eager to find out what was making her now visibly upset. Without saying a word, she finally reached into the envelope she was holding, and one after another started laying down on the consult room table, her son Devon's school portraits that she had picked up earlier that day.

"I always had a problem with my teeth's appearance," she continued, "I never smiled growing up, and I learned to cover my teeth with my hand whenever I was in public. I was so self conscious of my smile I hated having my picture taken, it was a horrible feeling going through school like that... and I never wanted my son Devon to suffer like me. As he was growing up, I knew Devon would have my crowded teeth, that's why I invested in braces for him for the last two and a half years, this was never supposed to happen...." She explained as she pointed at her son's straight face and almost puckered lips in the school portraits, and holding back the tears.

It was obvious that mom was having to relive her own painful past by seeing her son Devon conscious of his smile. It was even more disheartening for her to have invested time, effort and money into braces to fix the problem but to no avail! Initially, it seemed like Devon's less than perfect smile before braces had translated into a learned behavior that--if you've ever had a less than perfect smile--you can identify with. Behaviors like hiding the teeth by not opening your mouth when you smile, or just covering your mouth with your hand whenever in public could easily become a habitual pattern after a lifetime of practice.

After a brief chat with mom, I went back to the operatory to meet Devon. A very well dressed tall and slender young man in his late teens and a junior at the local high school, with aspirations to be an accountant. His small rounded glasses sat neatly centered on his face, perfectly complimenting his shy demeanor.

Initially, I was convinced that his lack of smiling was because of a learned habit, and that all I needed to do was to teach him how to gain back his confidence and grin ear to ear.

After a thorough examination, and analysis of the set of intra-oral and facial photographs, I handed a mirror to Devon and asked him to describe what he saw in his own words, and very quickly I realized I was dead wrong!

Devon's case proved much more involved than I head originally anticipated. His lack of smiling was not due to a past learned habit from before braces, but it was still a very real and conscious decision reinforced by a less than ideal smile, even after braces! The truth is Devon's after braces smile, may have been "good enough" for most teenagers, after all his teeth were straight, and bite was good... however, its wasn't good enough for Devon or his mom.

"My teeth are too small and they look like chiclets, and my canines look like vampire teeth..." he explained with the mirror still in his hand. Indeed, Devon was correct, and while he struggled to express his concerns in words, his assessment was indeed dead-on. In fact, what Devon didn't realize is that he had stumbled upon the Nine Golden Principles of a perfect smile, or what we typically refer to as the Recurring Esthetic Dental Proportions, or "RED" proportions for short.

In dealing with hundreds or maybe thousands of patients like Devon in the trenches of everyday dental practice, and through the analysis of what it takes to really make a smile dazzle, cosmetic dentists have identified nine key proportion principles that create a "stand out" smile. In my practice, we've memorized these principles to heart and use them in a checklist format for any patient contemplating esthetic enhancements to their smile.

These Golden Proportions, however are not new. They were used in ancient Greek architecture and in the great art of the ages. They can be observed throughout nature and the human body. Some of these principles are even used in modern building construction, car design and fashion. The balance and harmony they create are quite pleasing to the eye, and congruent with nature. Cosmetic dentists, using these same Golden Proportions, can find themselves creating that same balance and harmony between the smile, the face and a patient's personality. The nine principles are as follows:

1. Front Tooth Width/Height Ratio

Often when the front incisor teeth appear short and fat, tall and skinny, we may be dealing with a width/height discrepancy. The width/height ratio for each tooth should be around 77%. This can be simply calculated by using a millimeter ruler and measuring the length/height and width of the front incisor tooth on a close up photograph. For example if the width of the front teeth are 8.0mm and the height is 10mm, then the ratio would equal 80%, which is just about right. However, in Devon's case the teeth were 8mm wide and only 8 mm tall, and so the ratio was 100% or a square, which perfectly explains the "chiclets" look he placidly despised!

2. Color, Shading, Stains, and Markings

Are the teeth a uniform bright color or shade? Is one tooth darker than the rest? Are there white or dark spots or markings on the enamel? The brightness of a smile comes from the way the natural light reflects and refracts off the surface of the teeth. Any discrepancy in shade, stain or even surface texture of the tooth can translate to the imperfections often seen in self portraits or family photos. Devon's oral hygiene with the braces may have not been the best, and that left visible chalky-white rings on the enamel around his braces. The unevenness in the color of the teeth after the braces were removed became quite obvious.

3. The Smile Line

The smile line is, in essence, the amount of teeth show-ing when lips are at rest or with a very slight smile. Most young adults, including Devon should show around 2 mm of their upper teeth when their smile is at rest or with a casual or slight smile. As we age, this amount decreases as the front teeth wear down and/or the facial tissues begin to sag or lower down the face revealing more of the bot-tom teeth. Also, the incisal edges of the upper front teeth ("the smile line") should follow along with the contour or position of the lower lips when you smile. If the smile line doesn't, if it's flat or is actually inverted, it is referred to as a "reverse smile line". While my patients often refer to it as the "vampire smile," it is quite nicely correctable with porcelain veneers or bondings, unless of course you're into the whole Halloween-vampire scene!

4. Gum Line Symmetry

The gum tissue frames the teeth and sets the stage for the pearly whites to shine. Balance and symmetry of the gums are important parts of what makes an attractive smile. Is the height and scalloping of the gum line symmetrical or matched evenly between the left and right sides?

5. Gaps, Spaces and Diastemas

A "diastema" is a gap between teeth that are normally touching side by side. Often when teeth are positioned apart, small dark triangles form between the teeth where the gum tissue becomes shorter. Again, these are typically evident in photos, and often mistaken for dark stain or decay between the teeth!

6. The "Gummy" Smile

A gummy smile is when too much gum tissue shows above the front teeth while smiling. How much gum tis-sue shows with a full happy smile? Ideally there should be only a slight amount (1 to 3 mm) of gum tissue showing above the front teeth when you smile. Anything more than that detracts from a smile's appeal.

7. Horizontal Plane

The bite-plane is the plane or level formed by the biting surfaces of the teeth. A flat ruler held between the teeth and extending left and right beyond the cheeks would demonstrate this horizontal plane. This plane should not be canted with one side up or down, but should be parallel to an imaginary line drawn between the irises of the eyes.

8. Golden Proportion Ratio

This is one of my favorite rules that often gets missed. The front teeth sizes need to be proportionate to each other. The Golden Proportion follows the "rule of thirds." Each tooth away from the midline should be two-thirds as wide as the previous tooth as viewed from directly in front. For example lateral incisor measurement should be the 'visual' width when viewed straight on from the front, and not a side view. The central incisor should be 1.6 times as wide as the lateral incisor, and the canine 0.6 times as wide as the lateral – as the eye perceives it.

9. Vertical Dimension

Occlusal Vertical Dimension (or OVD) is simply the distance between the gums of the upper front teeth to the gums of the lower front teeth. The loss of vertical dimension, often due to clenching and grinding, makes your face appear older than it really is. Many devices, lotions, and creams, and even surgeries are currently used to erase and overcome the effects of aging. However, much of these aging effects are caused by decreased "vertical dimension" of the lower part of the face. As a rule of thumb, the measurement between the gum line of the top incisor and the gum line of the bottom incisor when biting on your back teeth should be somewhere between 17-21mm. For most people this creates a vertical proportion to the lower 1/3rd of the face that is esthetically pleasing and functionally healthy for the jaws and jaw joints.

As it turns out, Devon had a very acute sense of what his smile ought to look like, and rightfully so. His mom, on the other hand, could not quite understand why even after braces he was still covering his mouth when he smiled! After a long discussion with both of them about the Nine Golden Principles, and what they meant for Devon, we developed a game plan that included whitening, 6 porcelain veneers and some minor laser gum re-contouring. The results were outstanding and they were both thrilled!

Devon's story is unique but not uncommon. In fact, it happens more often than we like to admit. Often young people (and their parents!) have expectations that are not met, even after braces. This doesn't take away from the importance of orthodontic treatment for oral health and function, but meeting the esthetic expectations of patients like Devon is critical to the success of any cosmetic dental enhancement. In fact, after fifteen years in practice, I have realized that understanding and communicating expectations is the number one factor that affects how often patients like Devon show off their pearly whites!

About Dr. Hisham Kaloti

Dr. Hisham Kaloti is a dental artist who relies on conservative procedures to enhance the Health, Function, Beauty and Rejuvenation of smiles. His expertise in blending the science of dentistry with his artistic ability allows him to create natural appearing smiles on hundreds of people from all over the world, so they can look and feel their best.

A graduate of the University of Michigan School of Dentistry, he is also a Fellow and member of the International Congress Of Oral Implantologists, and a member of the American Academy of Cosmetic Dentistry.

Dr. Kaloti was the founder and served as the Chief Operating Officer of Dental Reflections, a dental chain with locations throughout the Midwest. He is an accomplished best selling author and international lecturer on the topic of cosmetic dentistry. He is also the recipient of the Donald A. Kerr Oral Pathology Award, the 2007 and 2010 Kids Connection Award. He has also served as the Regional Coordinator of the New Dentist Alliance, training dentists about the latest dental technologies and procedures.

His research related to dental implants was published in the journal of the National Institute Of Dental Research. Dr Kaloti has been the dentist of choice for over 10,000 patients over 15 years in 4 states and two provinces! His passion for creating one-of-a-kind smiles has been featured on NBC, CBS, ABC and FOX affiliates.

Dr. Kaloti dedicates time every year to conduct a Dental Makeover Contest where the winner receives up to $100,000 worth of cosmetic dentistry *pro bono.* He also dedicates time to providing dental care to impoverished communities in Haiti, Mexico, and Somalia through the Kaloti Foundation, a nonprofit organization dedicated to improving children's oral health world-wide.

CHAPTER 7

Periodontal Disease
—What You Must Know, and Why You Must NOT Get it!

By James D. Thomas, DDS

As a practicing general dentist, I have many patients that complain of painful gums, swollen gums and bleeding gums. Some people even think that it's normal for the gums to bleed. It is NOT normal for your gums to bleed.

I have two patients in my practice, I'll call them Susie and Bob (not their real names). Suzie and Bob chose two radically different courses of treatment for their dental problems.

Susie, at a younger age, decided that her troubled teeth were not worth keeping and decided to have all of her teeth extracted. She then had dentures made and she was miserable. Life for Susie was cumbersome with her teeth. She owns her own business, and is in the public eye all day long. She was embarrassed about the way her teeth fit, the way they felt, and how her teeth looked to her. She was not confident speaking with her dentures and constantly put her hand in front of her mouth. Suzie used to wear a lot of denture adhesive. Because her dentures did not fit well, the denture adhesive was required just to keep them in her mouth.

The first time Susie came to my practice she was already wearing a bad set of dentures. Because she had lost all of her teeth, the bone that supports the teeth had also been dissolved away by the body. Since there was almost no bone left to support the dentures, the dentures had no ridge of bone to rest on and would move all over her mouth. Working with an oral surgeon, we placed dental implants and did selective bone grafting to give us something to hold on to. After making new dentures over the dental implants, then Suzie could finally function in an almost normal matter. Whenever Susie comes in to my practice, I wonder to myself: what would life have been like for Susie, had she kept her teeth? Susie now has beautiful teeth and a wonderful smile of which she is proud. Her dentures stay in place and she's confident when working with the public. However, she went through a lot of misery. In addition, she will have to maintain her dentures - have them relined and periodically replaced for the rest of her life. I wish Susie would have come to see me before she had all of her teeth removed. I like to think that I may have made a bigger difference in her life and prevented a lot of the problems that she has had.

Bob chose a different course. Bob decided that he was going to keep his teeth. Bob works at a car dealership as a car salesman. When Bob first came to see me, he complained that a tooth or two were bothering him. He also complained that he often had bad breath and he was concerned about selling cars to the public when he had bad breath. As soon as I looked in Bob's mouth I knew we had big trouble. His gums were swollen and red and his breath was atrocious. My staff and I completed a thorough exam, including measurements of the gum pockets, x-rays and complete dental charting. I set Bob's chair up and we had a heart-to-heart talk. "Bob," I said, "you have periodontal disease, and you have it bad." We discovered that he had very deep gum pockets around a few of his molars, and many of the other measurements were not as bad, but were still very unhealthy. I recommended to Bob that he see a Periodontist, a dentist who specializes in treating periodontal disease. Because of the extent of the disease in his mouth, I felt that treatment by the specialist was the most appropriate course of action in order to give him the best result. Bob really did not want to go to another dentist. He was fearful of dentists and had become comfortable with our office. He questioned if there was any way that he could continue to come to our office and have the treatment done there. After some discussion, we decided that extracting the few bad molars would most likely be inevitable, even if he were seen by the specialist. If we extracted the bad molars, the rest of the mouth would have only moderate periodontal disease and we could easily treat that at our office.

With the patient excited to get his mouth healthy, we proceeded to run our complete testing protocol including bacteria DNA tests to determine which of the "bad" bacteria (the ones that cause periodontal disease) were present in his mouth and the amount of each present. We tested his DNA to determine his genetic tendency to develop periodontal disease. We had his blood sugar tested and C reactive protein checked as well, since these are related to periodontal disease and the health of the gums.

Bob then returned for several visits to treat the periodontal disease. This included deep cleaning while his mouth was numb, the use of dental lasers to kill the bacteria and enhance the healing of the gum tissue, and other treatment done in the office. In addition we gave Bob the tools he needed at home to help keep his gums healthy and continue the healing process from the treatment he was undergoing at our office. These involved mechanical devices, nutraceutical supplements, a special toothpaste and mouthwash and reinforcement about good home care. Bob took up the challenge and decided he was going to have a healthy mouth. We educated Bob about the correct eating habits, the types of food to eat, and the types of foods to avoid. We helped instruct him in the proper use of floss, toothbrushes, inter-dental brushes, and the other home-care tools he was taking home with him.

What was the result? After treatment, Bob had a healthy mouth. His mouth was looking good and he no longer had bad breath. His gum pockets were all normal and he had no bleeding gums at all. Bob is confident when selling cars now. He can talk at a closer distance with his potential customers and feels no shame or embarrassment about the way his teeth and gums look and is not afraid of how his breath smells. Unfortunately, Bob did have to lose a few teeth. However, unlike Susie, he has most of his teeth and he can chew better and does not have to worry about dentures or denture adhesives. Like Susie, I often wonder about Bob. I wonder what would've happened if he would've come to me before he got periodontal disease. Even if he had come before the periodontal disease had gotten really bad, his life would have been much better.

Like Susie and Bob, I have many patients with some form of periodontal disease. According to the American Dental Association, as many as 85% of adults have some form of periodontal disease. This is a horrifying figure. Recent research has shown that periodontal disease is linked to many other health problems. We have known for many years that the mouth is the gateway to the body. What you put into your mouth and how you care for your mouth can, and will, affect your general health. Because of recent research we know there are even stronger correlations than we had thought before. Studies have suggested a link between periodontal disease and heart attack, stroke, diabetes, certain types of cancer, and pregnancy complications. When I first started practicing dentistry and I would examine patients that had periodontal disease, I actually would tell them: "You have periodontal disease. It's bad, but you won't die from it." I can no longer tell that to my patients. A stroke or heart attack can actually kill you! It is imperative that you don't get periodontal disease. And if you have periodontal disease, it is imperative that you get it treated. Recent studies have concluded that treating periodontal disease lowers the risk factors for other health problems.

Here are seven things you must know about Periodontal Disease:

1. **For almost everyone, periodontal disease can be prevented or treated**. Benjamin Franklin once said, "An ounce of prevention is worth a pound of cure." Nowhere is that more true than in dentistry. Preventing gum disease and tooth decay is 'way' easier than treating either. That being said, periodontal disease can be treated and should be treated. Getting it in the first place should be avoided at all cost.

2. **Periodontal disease is caused by bacteria.** Scientists believe that there are as many as 400 to 500 different strains of bacteria in our mouths. They have identified 11 bacteria that cause periodontal disease and we actually have a DNA test for each of those 11 – and can determine if you have them, and relatively how much of them you have in your mouth. This DNA test is very useful for diagnosing periodontal disease, and then retesting at various points in the future to ensure that those bad bacteria are not recolonizing in our mouth.

3. **Great new treatment protocols have just recently been developed**. We now use specific wavelength lasers in dentistry as well as other proven protocols to help enhance the treatment and prevention of further periodontal disease. Lasers have been a wonderful addition in our arsenal of tools against periodontal disease. We routinely use dental lasers to help kill the bacteria and enhance healing in healthy patients as well as using it differently to treat periodontal disease in a proven protocol. Having used lasers in my dental practice for about seven years now, I have noticed that the patients who routinely undergo the laser prevention program have much healthier mouths. They have less gum pockets that are deep and they have less or no bleeding on probing when we check the gum pockets.

4. **Periodontal disease never gets better on its own**. It always gets worse. It needs to be treated. Although periodontal disease is common, it is not normal. Sometimes we injure a part of our body and rather than seeking medical care we wait for it to "heal". The only way that periodontal disease is "healed" is for the teeth to fall out of your mouth. Some people actually allow this to happen. When a tooth gets real loose they pull the tooth out themselves. This is often very painful and unnecessary.

5. **Our gums should never bleed.** Periodontal disease causes our gums to bleed. Bleeding gums are dangerous, because they allow the bad bacteria in our mouth to get into our bloodstream and infect the rest of our body. Our gum should never bleed – even when we brush and floss.

6. **Periodontal disease, at first, never bothers us**. However, in more advanced stages, periodontal disease can make our lives miserable. It often leads to painful abscesses, difficulty chewing, and swelling in our gums and face. An abscessed tooth is not only painful and disruptive to our daily schedule, but can actually be life-threatening. People have died from abscessed teeth, even in recent years.

7. **Proactive people generally have a healthier mouth.** I have seen over the years that patients who are proactive and active in their oral care have healthier mouths. They come to their dental appointments regularly, they are diligent and faithful about brushing and flossing and having good oral home care. They eat the right kinds of foods, and avoid foods that are bad for their mouth and body, and generally, they don't smoke.

If you want to have a healthy mouth, and subsequently, a healthier body, be proactive about your oral health. I can't tell you how many times a day I tell patients, "You need to brush your teeth more and you need to brush them longer." Brushing, flossing, and not smoking are the three most important things a person can do to have a healthy mouth. Regular dental visits are imperative. There are areas in your mouth that you cannot clean. A dental hygienist or dentist needs to clean your teeth regularly.

While you are at the dental office you should at least be screened for the red group bacteria - the most pathogenic of the 11 bacteria that cause periodontal disease. At our office we have a BANA test that can be done in minutes to screen for the red group bacteria. If this is positive, then we recommend further and more detailed testing and treatment for periodontal disease. Only your dentist can diagnose periodontal disease so please visit your dentist regularly.

Although I'm not a specialist, my general dental practice has helped hundreds, if not thousands of people live healthier, happier lives. There is nothing more rewarding to me than helping people in need and seeing them change for the better. Every day I get up and want to go to work to see who else we can help, and where we can make differences in people's lives. If you live in our area and are interested in finding out more about the health of your mouth, please contact us. We would be happy to meet you and give you specific detailed diagnostic information about your oral condition and how you can best have a healthy mouth. If it is impractical to visit us, please find a dentist near you who is using advanced diagnostic and treatment protocols to get the best results in combating this common but harmful disease.

About Dr. James Thomas

James D. Thomas, DDS has practiced general dentistry in Cass City, MI since 1996 after graduating from The University of Detroit Mercy, School of Dentistry. He has two degrees in Biomedical Engineering – a Bachelor's degree from Case Western Reserve University, and a Master's degree from Virginia Commonwealth University.

He has been interested in periodontal disease and how to treat it most effectively since his early days in Dental School. When graduating from Dental School, he was awarded the Periodontal Achievement Award for the student who had shown the most progress in periodontal studies and patient care.

Because of the progressive nature of periodontal education and treatment for his patients, he was contacted by the Centers for Dental Medicine and was offered the opportunity to join them as a "Center for Dental Medicine." Using their proven protocol of advanced diagnosis and treatment for periodontal disease, he has helped many of the area residents have healthier mouths and lives.

Being fascinated with technology and how it can benefit patients, he is regularly introducing new dental technologies that enhance diagnosis and outcome of treatment. In conjunction with digital radiographs that reduce radiation exposure, he also routinely utilizes soft tissue and hard tissue lasers to maximize treatment outcome while providing a comfortable patient experience.

Doctor Thomas lives in Cass City with his wife and eight-year old daughter.

If you would like to contact him or learn more about how you can receive the free Special Report "Periodontal Disease: 6 Key Ways to Know if You Have It," e-mail Doctor Thomas at casscitytoothdoc@gmail.com. You can also visit his website at: www.ASmileForLife.com .

CHAPTER 8

My Six Big Dental Connections That Couldn't Be True

By Dr. Henry (Brad) Bradford III

We often forget that the teeth and oral health are directly related to overall body health. Except where noted, the dental connections that follow are made from my own observations. To get you started, you must accept that the body is a terrific puzzle. Who ever figures it out, WINS!

1. THE MATERIALS USED TO RESTORE YOUR TEETH/MOUTH COULD BE CAUSING YOU PROBLEMS!

Many years ago, when certain metals were first coming out and being touted as the next best thing, one of my patients needed a bridge. At the time, we simply requested that the lab make us a porcelain-over-metal bridge for the patient. I like to double check the day after a large restoration is placed so imagine my surprise when she started complaining that something just didn't feel right. She said she was very irritable and that she just wanted to reach in and yank the bridge out. I double and triple checked the bite but saw nothing. More importantly, she showed no signs of irritation on the gums that might have indicated an allergic reaction. Finally, after a week of her complaining, I contacted the lab and had them make me a ring for her finger out of the exact same material the bridge was made out of. She called me the afternoon she started wearing the ring and said she couldn't tolerate it being on her finger! The second we removed the bridge from her mouth, she said she felt like a new person. To make sure it didn't happen again, we used a different metal to make the next bridge, but made a ring for her to wear prior to making the bridge. She was fine the day we glued it in and has been ever since.

Is it possible that a restoration placed in your mouth could cause something similar? Yes, but you should consider very carefully how long it's been a problem. I'd say the possibility increases if "It's just never felt quite right." So, how can you find out? Many labs send a slip stating what the restoration is made from so you at least have a starting point. Still, you have to be wary of disreputable labs and any potential for overseas outsourcing, since with them, you cannot be 100% sure of what you might be getting. In the event that all other avenues have been exhausted, have the dentist contact the lab to find out exactly what type of materials were used. You can always do as we did and have a ring or penny-like piece made from the exact same material. All it takes is wearing it or sometimes, holding it in the patient's mouth to provide dramatic feedback about that person's ability to tolerate that material.

Until we have an exact duplicate for enamel, there will always be the potential for patients to have reactions to the materials we use. There are some dentists and other healthcare professionals who propose the use of biologic testing to find out which materials the patient stands the best chance of tolerating. Biologic testing is a blood test – which determines which types of materials should work best in the patient. But, just like everything else, sometimes a small test of a material on a very sensitive patient can prove incredibly valuable before any sizeable investment in dental restorative work is made.

2. KIDS CAN BECOME VERY SICK FROM DENTAL PROBLEMS, BUT NOT REALLY COMPLAIN ABOUT PAIN.

"My kid just isn't herself. Not running a temp and nothing really hurts, but she feels bad, and the Drs. can't find anything wrong with her. I can tell you for sure that she's just not behaving normally. Could a dark tooth cause that type of problem?" This is the gist of the question/statement one parent posed. After taking a look at her, we determined that there was indeed an abscess, removed the tooth, and within two days she was back to her normal self.

Normally, a significantly dark tooth is an indicator of internal nerve trauma that has resulted in some form of bleeding within the root of the tooth. Often times, it happens after a fall, a bump, an elbow, or many other types of trauma to the front teeth. In most cases, the tooth or teeth involved develop an abscess in such a way that it may not hurt, but the infection continues to grow under the gums. This infection should be viewed as being as significant as any other infection anywhere in the body. Left untreated, it is potentially life-threatening given the right circumstances. Only dental x-rays can show an abscess of that nature, and this is one reason a complete series of x-rays or a panoramic x-ray should be taken every 3-5 years. If you have a child with a discolored baby tooth, it should be checked closely at regular dental visits. My recommendation is also that it be x-rayed at least once per year until it is lost. Abscesses have the potential to affect the developing permanent tooth as well as the overall health of the child. This is one time where early detection is extremely important. Children only develop once.

3. MY TOOTH IS CAUSING A PROBLEM WHERE?

A while back, I treated a patient by performing a root canal. It was a pretty unremarkable treatment and looked excellent on the x-ray when we were finished. The next time we were to take x-rays, about 6 months later, I had one of our great team members take an x-ray of that tooth as well. To my surprise, the abscess had gotten larger. So, we redid the root canal thinking there might have been something that just didn't work quite right. Six months later, with the abscess still growing, we redid it for the second time. All of the time we were working on the tooth, there was no indication that he was in pain. His only sign was an increasing size of the abscess when viewed on the x-ray. At one point, after the second redo, I asked him again how the tooth was feeling. His reply was, "The tooth feels fine, but my feet have started really hurting. So much so that I can't dance." Although you can't get much further away in the body than a top tooth to the feet, I asked that he wait until after we surgically removed the abscess to see a foot specialist. That abscess was particularly bad, but following its removal, and direct application of antibiotics with the bone replacement, his foot pain went away and has not returned since.

Simply a coincidence? It's possible. But with the many ways that bacteria or the toxic by-products they produce can travel within the body, all that is needed is a suitable location for the bacteria or toxins to land and cause disease. Have you ever heard a physician say, "we removed the tumor, but we don't think it was the origin of the problem?" In this sense, cancer cells and toothborne problems can behave very similarly. I've even seen a patient who got a prostate infection EVERY time he had his teeth worked on! Some physicians have now started referring patients back to their dentists for a full mouth x-ray series if they have infections in other parts of the body – which don't follow the normal rules or continue to return. It is great to see that more health professionals are drawing the connection between dental health and overall health. If you have any persistent infections anywhere in your body, it is very important to have your teeth checked with a complete series of x-rays looking for both tooth and gum abscesses or other problems.

4. MIGRAINES AND OTHER HEADACHES MIGHT BE DENTAL IN ORIGIN?

Many years ago, while talking to a friend, I found out that he was suffering from a severe headache that he'd had for almost a week. He had been to the emergency room, had an MRI, CAT scan, and tried several different medicines to no avail. I asked why he hadn't told me sooner and he said he didn't think it could possibly be dentally related. The next day we had him in the office, made him an appliance called an NtiTss and by that evening, he was pain free. After that he began regular splint therapy and had not had a headache problem since. He was so excited about being relieved from the headache that he and I went on a local total health talk radio show to help educate other potential sufferers about the possibility that their pain could be coming from their teeth or chewing system.

Unfortunately, a persistent headache is often misnamed a migraine headache. While there are many people who suffer from true migraines, there are many more who start as something much less severe and easier to treat. It's extremely important to know that headaches in general can be caused by many different sources. Pinched nerves in the neck, muscle spasms, increases in vascular pressure, swelling from a trauma, cancerous growths within the head, as well as many other origins can trigger a headache. Often times, a headache that starts in the temple region or seems to start deep within the cheek can be caused by a bite problem, made worse by clenching or grinding of the teeth. The muscles get into such tremendous spasm that the pain is excruciating and can begin to spread over the entire head. It's kind of like a Charlie Horse in the head. The remedies for this type of headache can sometimes take the pain away very quickly. Only a comprehensive examination of the head and neck muscles and the bite can tell for sure if the origin of a migraine is dental in nature.

How significant of a change can this make in a person's life? Well, while at a patient's baby shower, I had the patient's husband enthusiastically thank me for getting rid of his wife's headaches. To which I smiled and jokingly said, "You're welcome, but I hope you aren't saying I'm responsible for this baby."

5. YOUR GUMS COULD BE KILLING YOU!

No discussion on total body health would be complete without discussing one of the hottest topics in dentistry: The correlation between coronary artery disease and periodontal disease. Periodontal disease is an inflammatory disease in which an overgrowth of bacteria produces toxic byproducts – which create an increased permeability of the gums and a dissolution of the bone that holds the teeth in the mouth. In a nutshell, excess plaque in your mouth makes the gums so soft that the bugs can get into the rest of the body while the jawbones dissolve. There are several theories as to how gum disease contributes to coronary artery disease. The oral bacteria have been found stuck to the coronary artery lining of some patients blood vessels.(1)

The incidence of heart disease has also been shown to be higher in patients with periodontal disease. While much of the evidence does point toward there being a cause and effect relationship between gum disease and an increased risk for stroke or heart attack, a direct link has not been proven.(2)

Since it is not ethical to give someone gum disease and see if they have a heart attack or stroke, we may never know with 100% certainty. But, I can tell you that we never want any of our patients to have any signs of gum disease. It just isn't worth the risk.

6. MY MEDICATION CHANGED....NOW, I HAVE TMJ?

I was right in the middle of a complex restorative case with a particular patient and taking extra care to make sure that he did not develop any TMJ issues or headaches. All of a sudden, one day, the patient returns saying that his physician told him he has developed TMJ and should see his dentist. It took some extensive digging but we finally figured out that this patient had recently had his blood pressure medication changed, not because it wasn't working, but because there was a cheaper but just as effective alternative. To make a long story short, there was no way that I was going to accept that he had suddenly developed this condition while being so closely watched. In the end, the patient went back on his original medication and his TMJ/headache problem mysteriously disappeared.

Our bodies are magnificent creatures. They have an unbelievable ability to repair themselves and to adapt to new medications, or conditions. BUT, when something suddenly changes such as a new medication, new toothpaste, new favorite drink, etc., it can cause many different problems, sometimes even presenting as tooth related. Know your own body. Figure out if something recently changed. Perhaps the fix is nothing more than something to undo.

In conclusion, if you have any of those unusual symptoms that I've mentioned above, or even some other type of symptom that no one can get a handle on, don't hesitate to call your dentist and have him/her do a complete examination including full mouth x-rays, panoramic x-ray, diagnostic photos, and a thorough oral cancer screening. Your overall health depends on it.

References:

(1). American Academy of Periodontology website:
http://www.perio.org/consumer/mbc.heart.htm

(2). The American Journal of Cardiology and Journal of Periodontology Editors' Consensus: Periodontitis and Atherosclerotic Cardiovascular Disease. V. E. Friedwald, J. S. Kornman, J. D. Beck et al. Journal of Periodontology, July 2009

About Dr. Henry (Brad) Bradford III

Dr. Henry "Brad" Bradford III has been a practicing dentist for more than 20 years. He spent the majority of his career in the Greater New Orleans area practicing with his wife and partner, Dr. Sandra Catchings. He has been a part time instructor at the LSU School of Dentistry, prior to Hurricane Katrina. Following the storm, the health of their son deteriorated to the point that moving to a place far from a coastal environment was the only reasonable solution. In 2006, they moved to the Shenandoah Valley, living in Staunton, Virginia.

Dr. Bradford has given more than 40 speeches on dentistry to various business and civic organizations. He has written several articles and appeared on the New Orleans NBC affiliate station WDSU. He also has been featured on radio talk shows at stations WTIX and WKDW. He maintains a vibrant and growing practice with Dr. Catchings in Fishersville, Virginia, constantly noting the different dental challenges facing the two very different geographical locations in which he has practiced. They were the first to use CEREC technology and restore teeth with the ANKYLOS implant system in Augusta County, Virginia.

Their dental practice maintains an emphasis on total patient wellness while consistently working to stay ahead of the curve on new dental technology.

CHAPTER 9

Your Smile Can Help You Get The Three Things We All Want in Life: Health, Wealth, and Love
OR It Can Stop You Dead In Your Tracks

By Paul Eckstein, DMD

Mother Theresa was once quoted as saying, "Every time you smile at someone, it is an action of love, a gift to that person, a beautiful thing." I've seen it so many times in my 20 plus years of dental practice, how a smile can change a situation, disarm an angry customer, and even change a life.

My life definitely changed on August 17, 2010. It was a Tuesday morning and my office manager failed to show up for work. She was habitually a late person so we didn't think too much of it until a couple hours had passed and she hadn't answered or returned any of our calls or texts. I remember looking at the clock and it was 9:52 am when I got the news that Nicki had been murdered by her husband. Nicki was my office manager for 2 and a half years at that point, and had been my chairside dental assistant for three years prior to that. She was a close and trusted friend and one of the main reasons my practice was successful. My purpose here isn't to tell you about the circumstances surrounding Nicki's death. My purpose is to tell you about the changes that occurred after her death and how it changed my outlook on life, how I value the impact of a smile, and how Nicki's smile continues to impact the lives of others. You see Nicki and I made a decision one day about two years before she died. That decision was to come to the aid of a woman who had written us from prison. This woman, we'll call her Susan, had written over 50 dentists in Pinellas County Florida. We were the only ones that responded. Susan had been a crack addict and had been beaten by her boyfriend prior to her going to prison on drug charges. She was in a halfway house and was getting ready to be released when she wrote me. She only had four remaining upper teeth that weren't broken and needed something so she could smile, talk and go to a job interview with the hope of gaining employment. Nicki and I talked about the situation and decided that we would try to lend a hand any way we could. When Susan came to the office, even before we ever did anything for her, she was in tears because she was so grateful somebody would take a chance on her. Nicki talked with her in our consultation room for a few minutes before I saw her and Susan remarked how she would love to have a smile as pretty and white as Nicki's. In about six weeks time, we got her to where she had a removable partial denture that gave her the teeth back on top so she could smile without embarrassment. Now this isn't exactly cosmetic dentistry, but to Susan we may as well have done a $40,000 smile makeover for her. It was truly one of the most gratifying experiences of my professional career. Susan was determined to change her life for the better and went on to get a job working as a telemarketing agent. Not bad for someone who had a lisp and only four teeth just a month or so earlier. Her heartfelt letter to me is in my testimonial book in my reception area to this day.

After Nicki's funeral, I made a decision to honor her and help others by forming the Nicki Willman Foundation. The foundation is dedicated to giving victims of domestic violence free dental care. I saw firsthand the positive impact a smile can have on someone's life and how it can mean the difference between a life of fulfillment and a life of misery. The goal is to give these women a second chance and to help empower them through the power of a smile. (To meet Nicki and learn more about the Nicki Willman Foundation you can go to: www.edentalonline.com .)

Research has shown that people who smile more enjoy life more (not surprising), are more likeable and more fun to be around. They tend to exhibit less stress and they secrete less harmful hormones like Cortisol. People who smile more tend to have more energy and a more positive outlook on life and are generally viewed by others as being more successful. They are also viewed as being more trustworthy and they tend to be better off financially. A recent study even suggests that people who smile more live longer (on average about 7 years) than people who don't, and they have sex more often. If you aren't smiling as much as you should be, maybe you need a better smile to show off. The benefits are certainly clear. Your smile is your opening statement about who you are, a warning shot or 'shot across the bow' so to speak, about the person inside. It IS your first impression or lack of one when you enter a room, a meeting, or meet a new person. A beautiful smile speaks to confidence and charisma. It can be captivating. On the most superficial level it can say beauty or ugliness, and on a subliminal basis it speaks volumes about the person YOU want to project to the world. The benefits are actually priceless. If you were to find out today that you needed one of your legs amputated, what price would you be willing to pay to save your leg? Would you pay the same price for your teeth, for your smile? Would it depend on what insurance pays or would you come up with a plan and find a way to make it happen? If you believe that your smile is one of your best assets, let's explore:

THE FIVE STEPS TO TURN A BEAUTIFUL SMILE INTO A HEALTHIER YOU

1. Focus on the Foundation.

When I talk with patients at my office I often liken rebuilding their smile as similar to building a house. If you are going to build a mansion, you better have a solid foundation. In the mouth the foundation is the bone that supports the teeth and the tissue, gums and connective tissues that surrounds them. Over 70 percent of all Americans have some form of Periodontal Disease or "gum" disease. The links between oral disease and overall health are well documented and are discussed in other chapters of this book so I am not going to rehash it here. I am simply going to state that it is an imperative part of your oral and overall health plan. There is one simple task however; that you can implement that can make a dramatic improvement if performed daily.

This item is my "**Dirty Little SECRET** "so to speak. It is the **ONE** thing that if you implement will make the **MOST** difference in your oral and overall health. So here it is…

2. Buy and use an Oral Irrigator (Waterpik®).

The primary purpose of oral irrigation is to reduce harmful bacteria and ultimately the risk and severity of periodontal disease. Research has shown that using a Waterpik® or similar device on a daily basis can suppress harmful periodontal bacteria and their byproducts located within the sulcus or pocket. Practically speaking I just know that it works. As a cosmetic dentist anytime I do any type of bonding or all porcelain restorations like veneers and crowns I know that blood and saliva are my enemy to quality. It's like oil and water, it just doesn't mix. So if I have a person in 8 – 12 temporary crowns or veneers I insist that they use a Waterpik® during the 2 – 3 week period that they are in the temporaries. When they do this the results are fantastic. I have NO bleeding and the end results are always up to the patient's expectations.

So what does this mean for you? Quite simply that the daily use of a Waterpik® can be the difference between maintaining good oral health or having gum disease and periodontitis. It is not a cure all but it is the very best tool you can use every day to help in your fight against gum disease. When paired with professional care it quite simply works.

There are several types of irrigators on the market. My favorite is a pulsed flow irrigator and of these the base model Waterpik® is the best. It is only a $40.00 - $45.00 investment and does the best job. Next would be the Showerfloss® (www.showerfloss.com). It is preferred by some patients because of its ease of use and it is significantly less messy and is used in the shower. It can only be purchased online for around $25.00. If you use one of these daily, I guarantee you will see an improvement in your tissue health.

For instructions on how to use an oral irrigator properly go to: http://www.edentalonline.com/articles-1/example-dental-article

3. Have a Plan and a Budget.
Realize that your oral condition didn't get that way overnight and it may take some time to get everything back on track. In this immediate gratification society we live in, this can be a difficult concept for some people. The simple truth is that the body heals in its own time frame and all the best intentions in the world can't change that. Another fact is that the vast majority of dental problems cause little to no pain. When a patient has pain it is easy to recognize and typically easy to diagnose and treat. That's not to say it is simple to treat. Many times when a patient is in pain, it is because a problem has developed that is beyond what a simple filling or even a crown can fix.

My motto is "**Kill the Monster When It Is Little.**" This simply means fix the problem while it is small. It is typically easier and less costly in the long run and can often help you avoid procedures like root canals or an extraction and an implant. While these procedures are typically successful and sometimes a necessary part of a treatment plan, many times they can be avoided by early intervention. Large silver amalgam fillings for example, can be asymptomatic for years and appear fine. Over time however, cracks develop due to metal expansion and they can literally split the tooth down the middle and into the bone. Not only does this typically cause pain and a dental emergency situation, but also it is usually more expensive and extensive to fix. These problems and others like them can be detected and planned for in advance. Have your dentist help you clearly identify your goals and objectives.

Whether you want straighter teeth, whiter teeth, bigger teeth or all of the above, find someone that can develop a treatment plan for you to meet your needs. There are many financing options available these days. Realize that dental insurance will most likely NOT get you where you want to go, but it may help offset some of your expenses. Comprehensive dental treatment can be expensive but it is a worthwhile and fantastic investment. To quote Fred Joyal, founder of 1-800-DENTIST, **"What else can you invest in that will affect every smile, every kiss, every meal and every word you speak, every day for the rest of your life?"**

4. Straight Teeth are Healthy Teeth.

Did you know that crooked teeth have a higher incidence of periodontal problems than straight teeth? 74 percent of all Americans suffer from some type of malocclusion. Research has shown that even in people with otherwise healthy mouths, detrimental bacteria exists more often and in higher quantities in areas where teeth are crooked.

This can contribute to periodontal disease, traumatic occlusion, pain and eventually tooth loss. Some of this is due to a greater difficulty in cleaning crowded areas of the mouth. In addition, problems with the bite can lead to tooth fractures, problems with the jaw joint and even migraine headaches. Other benefits of straight teeth for patients are:

- The need for less restorative dentistry due to better cleaning ability

- Less need for more invasive dental procedures for cosmetics like crowns and veneers

- Easier and more effective plaque control and instrumentation for patient, dentist and hygienist

- Better bite and occlusion which means less TMJ (Temporomandibular Joint) problems and the problems associated with traumatic occlusion

- The obvious benefit of a **Straighter Healthier Smile**.

There are many alternatives for adult orthodontics making it easier than ever for you to have straight teeth. Traditional brackets and wires, 6 Month Smiles, and Invisalign clear braces are but a few. Your dentist can help you decide which option is best for you.

5. Buy and Use a Tongue Scraper.

Have you ever noticed a white or dark coating on your tongue? This is **not normal** and indicates an excess of bacteria, food debris, dead cell material, and volatile sulphur compounds. If you **have never used a tongue scraper let me be the first to warn you.** The first time you use it you will likely get a large amount of visible plaque, bacteria, and debris that is not pleasant. Much of this is from the VSCs (volatile suphur compounds) responsible for bad breath. 90% of all halitosis (bad breath) originates in our mouths, 80% comes from our tongue. Most comes

from the sulfur compounds that are produced on the pos-
terior portion of our tongue and from active periodontal
disease or tooth decay. In addition damaging bacteria can
live in the deep grooves of the tongue and can contribute
to worsen periodontal conditions. A tongue scraper allows
you to clean these areas and can also help improve the
performance of the taste buds making food more enjoy-
able. There are numerous types available on the market.
My favorite is the plastic Oolitt and is available through
your dental professional or online.

The benefits of a healthy mouth and a beautiful smile are numerous and go far beyond the pleasing appearance of straight white
teeth. My years as a practicing cosmetic dentist and the lessons
learned from Nicki and from helping others have provided me
countless examples of people who have benefited both mentally
and physically; improving not only their physical well being but
also improving their self esteem and self confidence. If you follow the five steps outlined here, you too will be well on your
way to having the smile of your dreams.

About Dr. Paul Eckstein

Paul Eckstein, DMD is the owner and founder of E Dental in Seminole, FL. He is a licensed practicing cosmetic dentist and is affectionately known as "Dr. E." by his patients. He is a 1991 graduate of The University of Pittsburgh School of Dental Medicine and a graduate of The Hillsborough County Dental Research Program in 1992.

In 2009 Dr. Eckstein was recognized by the Consumer Research Council of America as one of America's top dentists. In 2012 he was a Florida Top Doctor Awards Recipient and is also listed by the Heritage Registry of Who's Who in Dentistry in 2012.

Dr. Eckstein is also the founder of the Nicki Willman Foundation, a 501 (c)(3) Non-Profit Corporation dedicated to assisting victims of domestic violence by helping them rebuild their smiles. The Foundation was established in September of 2010 and gives free dental services to women in need. To learn more about Dr. Eckstein, E Dental or The Nicki Willman Foundation, go to: www.edentalonline.com or call (727) 319-6019.

CHAPTER 10

CAD-CAM DENTISTRY!
– TOO MANY PATIENT BENEFITS TO BELIEVE

By Donald Galbo, DDS

When I was a youngster the *modus operandi* of a dentist rarely included the concept of painless dentistry. I was tortured at every visit, and knew at a very early age that hurting patients would not be an option for me when I became a dentist. I was very lucky, as I knew at the age of twelve that I was going to be a dentist. It was my calling! I remember thinking how "barbaric" everything seemed to be on every visit to my dentist. The post WWII mentality didn't leave much concern for comfortable dental visits. Everything seemed like a torture. Nowadays, the young patients, who need treatment rarely have any thing to worry about in most practices. Surely, all the procedures being done to me could be handled better? Little did I know that technologies would evolve so rapidly that they would exceed even my wildest dreams. I remember watching the movie "2001, A Space Odyssey" and listening to Hal (the man in the computer). I was mesmerized by the possibility that computers might truly enhance the human experience. I was also intrigued by the medical advances proposed by "Star Trek". Medicine and Dentistry have made so many giant leaps from the precepts of those days already past, and so far off in the future. Well, 2001 is gone and

2320 is still a long way into the future. However, the human race has made great strides in our ability to treat our fellow humans in more efficient, successful, and humane ways. This chapter will highlight just one of those major advances in dentistry. It is my hope that this technique will become the standard of care in restorative dentistry, rather than the exception within the next five to ten years.

"This procedure gives the doctor total control over one day fabrication of all ceramic restorations for patients". Most patients to this day who have had any experience with having Crowns, Veneers and/or Bridges have had to go through the old standard procedures. That being impressions, temporary crowns, and a second visit to have the permanent work placed. That always meant another visit, which involves more time taken off by the patient, more travel and fuel used for the trip, and most likely another round of anesthesia. I'm not sure why any patient would accept the old procedure if they knew where they could find an experienced Cad-Cam dentist. "It is very satisfying to be able to do Cosmetic Procedures, such as all new front Crowns or Veneers in one day, and see the myriad of emotions" elicited. Many patients leave with tears in their eyes, and so appreciative for the life changing smile they have just received. You see, many patients would have had the cosmetic dentistry they need done earlier, if they knew they could escape the need to wear temporary crowns for weeks. Now when they find out about the one visit benefit the Cad-Cam technique provides, they are thrilled. They really love the fact that they do not have to walk around with those temporary crowns. What is still amazing to me as a practitioner, is the small percentage of dentists worldwide doing this amazing computerized fabrication of milled porcelain restorations. The latest estimates have it at around 13%. Very low, considering it was around 2% in 1998, when I joined the ranks of users. I really thought it would be more accepted by dentists by now. There is quite a good story to tell here. What things could be in play that would keep a dentist from making this change?

Patients can benefit from one day fabrication of crowns (caps) and now bridges made by a dentist trained and experienced in the rapidly evolving area of Cad-Cam Dentistry. As mentioned in my bio, I am one of the first dentists in the United States to be certified in the Cad-On Technique for making bridgework in one day (replacing missing teeth with permanently cemented or bonded dental work). This technique was researched and developed by Ivoclar Vivadent, a well-known and respected Ceramic manufacturing Company.

The Cad-Cam technology was introduced to the dental profession in 1985 as the Cerec 1 machine. It was very crude in it's ability to mill restorations, and could only do inlays to replace fillings, but still provided a very strong tooth-colored restoration with greater strength and longevity than the vast majority of composite resin fillings placed in those days. One of the reasons dentists have not embraced this technology is the cost. The first machine cost in the neighborhood of $100,000.00. Back then, it would take lots of porcelain inlays to make the machine cost effective, and most of the fillings were still done with silver amalgam. I decided to enter the Cad-Cam revolution in 1998, when the second machine, Cerec 2, was introduced. The Cerec 2 machine was now $64,000.00, and with the ability to do Crowns, Veneers and Inlays, it was possible to do these now cost effectively. There was still the outrageously arduous learning curve to contend with. While I had been watching the evolution of Cad-Cam technology, I wasn't convinced to embrace it until the software allowed the ability to do Crowns, and Veneers.

There have been some factors that have hampered the more rapid acceptance of the Cad-Cam Technique into more dental practices. First, the concepts that guide the art and science of Cad-Cam dental procedures is quite different from the way things are done utilizing a dental laboratory. In addition to shifting one's thought process, the learning curve in the early years of Cerec 1, 2 and even 3 was initially very steep. Unlike most commonplace learning curves where the progress is generally up, there was a steep dip in the learning curve that was very frustrating for most dentists to accept. Therefore, many practitioners would start off with a passion, but get stuck on the most tedious part of the learning, and push the machine aside into a corner of their office to collect dust.

Now, with the advent of significant advances in the computer hardware, computer operating systems, and the software, the acquisition of the necessary skills is becoming less intensive and frustrating. Sirona dental, the dental division of Siemens Medical, has spent thousands of hours and millions of dollars in the continuing research and development of their Cerec machines. The fourth installment of the machines, the Cerec AC (my third machine), now has the capacity to seamlessly produce crowns, inlays, veneers and bridges to replace missing teeth. Whether replacing these teeth with crowns on natural teeth or implant abutments, we can now confidently produce and place multiple unit bridges in a single day. This was always a dream of mine! I must say that the forward progress in Cad-Cam technologies has been at a rate never anticipated. Truly, I never thought we would have these types of tools in my lifetime. I couldn't even dream of the actual advances in my first five years let alone the last three to five years.

Over the last eight years or so, another machine, made by Sullivan-Schein Dental Supply Company has entered the market. The E4D Unit was refined over many years, and while the largest market share has been held and maintained by Sirona's Cerec Machine, the E4D has made some improvements of their own. I have always believed that competition is good for all free market-driven products and techniques. So, with the feedback from doctors using these devices, the ingenuity of the engineers working on them, and the computers that drive them, we march forward with what seems like never ending innovations. Just when I think things have gone as far as they could possibly go, the next significant advancement is introduced. I suspect that we, the human race, are just scratching the surface of what is possible to attain with technologies.

For those patients who have had to go through the standard impressions, making of temporary crowns, and having to return for their second visit, this technique is like a dream. No more four minutes of "gunk" in the mouth, followed by acrylic chemicals in the mouth to make a temporary crown, which tastes like a "nail salon" in the mouth. Unfortunately, depending on the skill and artistry of the dentist/assistant there is much variability in the appearance of temporary crowns, and they may or may not look natural. Now, with the Cad-Cam technique there is a ten second digital image or set of images over twenty seconds. Then, you the patient get to relax and watch the doctor do his magic. In some offices the assistants have been trained to do the bulk of the design work, with the doctor doing the final edits before milling of the restoration begins.

The next step is the selection of the proper material, the proper shade, and placing the proper size of the block of highly pressed and strengthened porcelain/ceramic into the milling chamber. Now, the crown, veneer, bridge, or inlay that has been designed is quickly milled into existence. During the milling process the data from the computer is streamed to the milling machine. Within three to ten minutes an inlay, crown or veneer is accurately produced. The bridgework takes longer to design and mill, and some types of bridges like the Cad-On can take hours to go through additional firing procedures. Many bridges today are made without any metal in them. This was not the case even ten years ago. A material, that many know as Cubic Zirconia (synthetic diamond) can be milled for a very strong, and highly esthetic base. Then porcelains can be added or milled to bond to the Cubic Zirconia base (which is the part that actually fits the teeth).

Finally, these new restorations are adjusted to fit properly, and bonded to the teeth with the most current generation of dental bonding adhesives. These new bonding agents seal the tooth structure in a way that earlier generations of cements could not. They bond stronger, seal the teeth better from potential sensitivity, and permit more esthetic results than ever before.

The process of adjusting shape and appearance is now done by the doctor or assistant in the office. In the past, when a dental laboratory was employed the process could take weeks. If the dental restoration came back with any problems, it had to go back to the laboratory. With the Cad-Cam techniques we are able to correct these problems on the same day. Of significant value to the dentist and the patient is that the data used to construct the restoration is saved by the computer, and can be recalled to produce the exact same restoration if needed in minutes. Just suppose that you had one of these crowns made for a front tooth and you had an accident that completely broke the crown, we can go to the computer, pull up the data, and have another crown waiting for you when you walk in the front door. The convenience of this recall and immediate fabrication of the original is tremendous, and not possible when using a dental laboratory. The use of a laboratory would require a new impression, temporary crown and weeks waiting again. Then, the dreaded second visit again.

Cad-Cam dental technology is one of the most useful, convenient, and significant advancements in dentistry since the profession began before the American Civil War.

About Dr. Don Galbo

Donald Galbo, DDS is an Internationally-recognized expert in the application of Computerized Dental Technologies. These technologies, while not widely embraced by the majority of dental professionals around the world, offer many exciting benefits to patients. Dr. Galbo has been a Member of the American Academy of Computerized Dentistry, The North American Academy of Computerized Dentistry, and the International Society of Computerized Dentistry. While he has embraced many other advanced technologies his primary passion has been with Cad-Cam dentistry. He has been a certified trainer and taught hundreds of new users in basic training and beyond. His thirteen years of operating experience have given him invaluable insight into how to effectively utilize this remarkable technique. He has fabricated over fifteen thousand restorations with his three different Cerec Cad-Cam units. Cad-Cam is the abbreviation for Computer Assisted Design-Computer Assisted Milling. He is one of the first dentists to be certified in the Cad-On Technique for the fabrication of bridgework in a single day.

He graduated Cum Laude from Mount Saint Mary's College (now University) in Emmitsburg, Maryland in 1976, with a B.S. Degree in Biology, and minor in Chemistry. While in the Pre-Med Curriculum there he was also elected to the Monsignor Teirney Honor Society. While at the University of Maryland School of Dentistry, in Baltimore, he was very active in the Student Dental Association, and served as Vice President (3), and President (4). He also was elected as the Senior Most Dedicated to his school and profession (The Kathryn Toomey Award). While in his senior year at this first dental school in the world (also known as The Baltimore College of Dental Surgery) he was awarded the Senior Thesis Award. He obtained his D.D.S. Degree in 1982. After a short stay at the dental school as a Clinical Instructor in the Department of Oral Medicine and Diagnosis, he spent three years as a Senior Assistant Dental Surgeon in the U.S. Public Health Service. Since his separation from that service in 1985 he has been in private practice in the Atlanta, Georgia area. When he is not doing dentistry, he enjoys playing basketball, and his other hobby where he is a DJ and Sound Engineer.

To see more of Dr. Galbo and his practice you may visit at:
www.northsidedentalofnewnan.com

CHAPTER 11

Can Cosmetic Dentistry Actually Change Your Life? –Smile More, Live More!

By Dr. Mariliza LaCap

Smiling...

I smile a lot. As far as I can remember, people have always complimented me on my smile..........this is good for me because I am a dentist. I never thought my smile made an impact on my life so I used to take my smile for granted...this was bad for me because, as a dentist, I never realized the value of a beautiful smile. And so my story begins........

I met my husband in dental school 25 years ago. He was my anatomy lab partner. Was it love at first sight? If you ask him, he'll give you a different version, depending on his mood. The truth is, he loved me from the time he saw me. I, on the other hand, fell in love with him over hours of studying and cramming for our Physics and Anatomy exams.

Unlike me, my husband never liked his smile. He felt self-conscious and insecure about his front teeth. Early on during our marriage, when he had enough confidence in me as a cosmetic dentist, he begged me to give him a smile makeover. We disputed over his makeover for a week. I felt his smile was nice enough for me to marry him......after all, who was he trying to impress? The reality is his smile was not that great. He fell on his front teeth at the awkward age of 7 during a soccer accident, leaving him with poorly made crowns on his four front teeth. The crowns were made by his childhood dentist who had no concept of cosmetic dentistry – which only proves that not all dentists are created equal.

My husband won the battle and I conceded to giving him a new and improved smile. The day I completed his smile makeover, we went out to dinner to celebrate his new smile. My husband was beaming from ear to ear. You couldn't take the smile off his face. After taking our order, our waitress turned to my husband and said, "You have a very nice smile!" My husband soaked in the compliment and basked in that one single moment all night with a big grin on his face. With sincere curiosity I asked, "What's the big deal? People tell me I have a nice smile all the time."

"You don't understand," said my husband. "I'm 36 years old and in all my life, no one has ever told me I had a nice smile". This night began my husband's transformation into a more confident, charismatic and outgoing individual.

Don't get me wrong, he was always confident, charismatic and outgoing on a one-on- one basis, but never in a group, social or work setting. My husband's new smile changed his life and my life. Because of his new smile, opportunities opened up to him. His passion for transforming people's lives through a "smile makeover" has been raised to new heights. After all, he was not just a cosmetic dentist; he was a walking testimonial of what cosmetic dentistry can do for you.

Can Cosmetic Dentistry Actually Change Your Life? Yes it can!

I truly believe if it wasn't for my husband's new smile, he would not be as confident, happy, charismatic and successful. Why is having an attractive smile so important? Here are some astonishing facts.

84 percent of adults perceive having an attractive smile as important, according to a survey conducted by Harris Interactive. This poll of 1,000 American adults between the ages of 18 and 50 years found that more than one-third would not be likely to set up their best friend on a blind date with someone with bad teeth.

In the same study, an overwhelming majority – 85 percent – considers a person's smile to be very or somewhat important when meeting someone for the first time. Almost 9 out 10 Americans polled said they thought people with good teeth are more attractive.

In an independent study conducted on behalf of the American Academy of Cosmetic Dentistry, virtually all Americans (99.7%) believe a smile is an important social asset.

In the same study, 96% of adults believe an attractive smile makes a person more appealing to members of the opposite sex.

Three-quarters (74%) of adults feels an unattractive smile can hurt a person's chances for career success. When asked, "What is the first thing you notice in a person's smile?" The most common responses were: Straightness, Whiteness & Color of Teeth, Cleanliness of Teeth, Sincerity of Smile and Sparkle of Smile.

"FIRST IMPRESSIONS ARE THE BIGGEST VALUE OF AN ATTRACTIVE SMILE"

When meeting someone for the first time, the way you look is even more important than what you say. Sociolinguist Albert Mehrabian found in his comprehensive research on communication that:

- 7 percent of a verbal message comes from the words used.

- 38 percent comes from the vocal tone, pacing, and inflection.

- 55 percent is transmitted by the speaker's appearance and body language.

Your smile is one of the first nonverbal cues you give to people. You may notice that other people treat you a certain way when they meet you, often without even talking to you. You may have also heard the phrase that "When you smile, the whole world smiles back at you." My husband was ashamed of how his teeth looked; he was embarrassed about his smile. This took away his confidence. The non-verbal cue of not smiling was read in a negative way.

When you don't smile because you are embarrassed of your teeth, people may think you have low self-esteem, that you have little confidence, that you're not capable of a more important job, or of sustaining a deep and lasting personal relationship.

A new smile can make you look better and younger, boost your self-confidence and self-esteem, as well as increase your communication ability, your sex appeal, and impact on your personal and professional relationships.

Now that you know what an attractive smile can do for you, what is the next step? The next step is choosing the right Cosmetic Dentist. When you choose the right dentist, getting that smile isn't as complicated as you might imagine.

Many people can have a dramatic change in their smile with just a few visits to the right dentist. So many options are available today that there is no reason why you need to suffer the injustice of an unattractive smile.

TOP 10 CRITICAL THINGS YOU SHOULD KNOW BEFORE YOU SELECT A COSMETIC DENTIST

Cosmetic dentistry is an investment in the future of your smile. And, like any investment, you'll want to do a little research before making a final decision. Reading this chapter is the first step. These guidelines can help you choose the dentist who's right for you.

1. Investigate the doctor's training. The best cosmetic dentistry practitioners didn't just go to dental school; they also completed extensive post-graduate training programs that focus specifically on issues of cosmetic dentistry. In addition, the best dentists regularly attend continuing education classes to stay up-to-date on new procedures and materials.

2. Start with a consultation and make sure the doctor under-stands you. Going in for a consultation is a great way to learn more about a dentist and dental practice. Consulta-tions are generally inexpensive, and are sometimes even offered for free. Talk to the dentist before you commit to anything. Remember, it's your job to make an educated decision.

3. Look for smile design experience. Cosmetic dentistry is as much art as it is science. In general, the more smiles a dentist has designed, the better that dentist's work will be. Smile design is about more than just your teeth; the dentist should also consider your lips, gum line, mouth shape and facial structure.

4. Communication is key. It's essential that you be able to talk to your dentist - and that your dentist will listen to you! There's a lot of dialogue that needs to go into an individual long-term treatment plan. If you feel bullied, pressured, or rushed, then that's probably not the right dentist for you.

111

5. Look at before and after photos. Take a look at the dentist's portfolio before you make up your mind. Pay specific attention to cases that are similar to yours. Make sure that the photos are of actual work done by the dentist, not just stock photos.

6. Watch out for very low prices. Some dentists try to make up for poor materials and shoddy work by offering low prices. You get what you pay for.

7. An honest dentist sets realistic expectations. Watch out for doctors who promise more than they can deliver. You want a dentist who will tell you what can and cannot be done for your smile. You need to know how long the process will take, what you'll have to do, and any complications that could occur.

8. Technology is cool, but it's not the only thing. A dentist with high-tech modern equipment is more likely to be up-to-date on modern techniques. At the same time, however, don't let yourself be dazzled by a dentist's fancy tools; what really matters is if the dentist knows how to use them properly.

9. A good lab technician is a valuable asset. The dentist might decide on the treatment plan, but it's the lab technician who'll actually fabricate the porcelain veneers or crowns that will be gracing your new smile. Great dentists are proud of their lab technicians and the materials they use.

10. Check out the facilities. Take a look around. What sort of equipment does the practice use? What is their sterilization process? Is it a comfortable atmosphere? Are the employees happy and helpful? Do they take the time to answer your questions?

Now that you've had a "Smile Makeover," let's start smiling more!

WHAT ARE THE 10 HIDDEN POWERS OF A SMILE?

1. A SMILE MAKES YOU MORE ATTRACTIVE. People are naturally drawn to those who smile. If you are looking to meet someone new, nothing will help as much as a genuine smile. A frown or glare pushes people away from you, while a big smile brings them in.

2. A SMILE TRICKS YOU INTO A BETTER MOOD. Feeling down? Force yourself to smile. When you smile, your body and mind will think you are in a good mood -- and pretty soon, you actually will be.

3. A SMILE BOOSTS YOUR IMMUNE SYSTEM. Some research has shown that smiling can affect your body's immune system, so when you relax and smile, you are also helping boost your immunity to disease and infection.

4. A SMILE LOWERS YOUR BLOOD PRESSURE. Because smiling relaxes you, it can also reduce your blood pressure and decrease stress. Whenever you get upset, take a deep breath and smile. You'll be surprised how quickly you can calm down and feel good again.

5. A SMILE REDUCES PAIN. Endorphins and serotonin are released when you smile. The endorphins are a natural painkiller (no wonder they say, "Grin and bear it.") while serotonin is a mood enhancer; so not only can you reduce pain, you can also get a natural high by smiling.

6. A SMILE MAKES YOU LOOK YOUNGER. Smiling works out your face muscles. Don't be afraid of laugh lines, a smile can actually improve your skin's elasticity and make you look younger.

7. A SMILE STOPS AN ARGUMENT. Whether you are arguing with your partner or with a co-worker, a smile can be all you need to diffuse the conflict. It lets the other

person know that you really aren't that angry and you aren't being defensive. Even a smiley face in an email can help deter an argument or break bad news.

8. A SMILE MAKES A CONNECTION. Whether you are eyeing a guy on a crowded subway, trying to get a waitress' attention in a busy restaurant or attempting to get assistance at the DMV, a smile can make the connection you need. A smile makes you so approachable that it can be your introduction to a person before you even say a word.

9. A SMILE CAN GET YOU A JOB. Smiling shows you are confident, warm and friendly. It can make a real difference in a job interview. If you were deciding between two candidates with equal skills, which one would you hire? The one with the frown or the one with the big, genuine smile?

10. A SMILE MAKES SOMEONE'S DAY. You never know what someone could be going through. They could be angry, upset or heartbroken. A smile across the room to a stranger may brighten his day and really make a difference in his life.

The world always looks brighter from behind a smile. ~ Author Unknown

About Dr. Mariliza LaCap

Dr. Mariliza LaCap is a cosmetic dentist who has been creating beautiful smiles through exceptional care in her Bergenfield, NJ office, Washington Dental Associates for over 20 years with her husband, Dr. Darren Tong. Dr. LaCap and Dr. Tong first met in dental school at Columbia University School of Dental and Oral Surgery. In fact they were anatomy lab partners. Was it love at first sight? You'll have to ask them.

After over 20 years of working together as dentists, they still share the same passion for creating beautiful and healthy smiles. Their shared vision for Washington Dental Associates has materialized into an exceptional dental experience for their patients.

The experience in their office and their dentistry is so exceptional that they are known as the "Mercedes Benz" of dentistry within their community. Washington Dental Associates is a unique dental office where patients feel comfortable, well taken care of, and safe.

Another passion they share together is their passion for each other and their five children. Their free time is spent watching their sons' soccer or baseball games - they have never missed one yet. Currently, the family's favorite destination is Disney World.

Dr. Mariliza Lacap received her D.D.S. degree from Columbia University School of Dental and Oral Surgery through an academic scholarship where she graduated in the top 10% of her class. She also received extra training in cosmetic dentistry at New York University Dental School. She completed her residency at Englewood Hospital.

Dr. LaCap has also received advanced training in Dental implants, Cosmetic Dentistry, Orthodontics, Full-Face Orthodontics, Invisalign™, Endodontics, Gum Disease, Patient Management, and Restoration.

Her professional affiliations and awards include:
Member: American Dental Association, New Jersey Dental Association, Academy of General Dentistry, Bergen County Dental Society, Bergen County Implant Study Group, International Congress of Oral Implantologists, and American College of Implantologists

Awards: Excellence in Orthodontic Award - American Association of Orthodontics; Excellence in Periodontics Award - Northeastern Society of Periodontists

CHAPTER 12

Pediatric Dentistry

By Isioma Anizor, DDS

As a general dentist I work with adults and children. One thing I have seen consistently is adults with missing teeth, poor dental health, and poor dental hygiene. When I ask these patients how they lost their teeth or why they lost their teeth, most of them report that they lost their first adult teeth when they were children. From there things went downhill. Our oral health is something we often take for granted. A healthy mouth enhances our ability to smile, speak, smell, taste, touch, chew, and swallow. It gives us self-confidence and enhances our ability to communicate with others. Tooth decay, periodontal disease and other oral diseases affect millions of Americans each year.

Good oral health is very important. For that reason, it is important to develop good oral health habits early. As we have been hearing over the past few years, our oral health is directly related to our overall health. With that in mind, I would like to discuss children's dentistry to allow you to prepare your children for a healthy future.

The Academy of Pediatric Dentistry recommends that children start routine dental visits by the age of one because oral health requires good home care and professional care. According to CDC statistics, over 19% of children between the ages of 2 to19 have untreated dental cavities.

According to the CDC, 500 million dental visits occur per year, but despite this fact, many children suffer from oral diseases that could be prevented. 20% of children ages 4 to 5 have tooth decay. By the third grade, that percentage goes to 50%, then by age 17, 86% of children are diagnosed with tooth decay.

The risk of dental disease can be greatly reduced with proper preventative care, regular dental checkups and dental care.

This chapter will give you the information you need to care for your child's teeth. Let's start with some of the most common questions I get from parents.

1. WHAT ARE CAVITIES AND WHY DOES MY CHILD HAVE CAVITIES? HE DOESN'T EAT CANDY.

Despite the fact that enamel is the strongest substance in the human body, tooth decay is one of the most common of all disorders, second only to the common cold. It usually occurs in children and teenagers, but can affect anyone. It is a common cause of tooth loss in younger people.

Cavities are holes in teeth formed when bacteria in your mouth use the sugar in food to make acid. This acid eats away at the teeth. When people hear that sugar causes cavities, they try to eliminate candy and sweets from their children's diets. What they don't know is that tooth decay occurs when foods containing carbohydrates such as breads, cereals, milk, fruits, cakes, or candy are left on the teeth. The combination of these foods with saliva, acid and bacteria forms plaque, which sticks to the tooth surface. Plaque begins to build up on teeth within 20 minutes after eating. If the plaque remains on the tooth surface for long enough it dissolves the enamel surface creating cavities.

2. WHAT ARE THE RISK FACTORS FOR CAVITIES?

There are certain population groups that are at increased risk for cavities: Children who live in communities without fluoridated water, children from families with low incomes, children from some racial and ethnic groups, children with limited or no dental insurance, children with special health care needs.

Another risk factor are children who have the following conditions: Preterm infants or birth weight infants, children with certain health conditions e.g., gastric reflux, children with obvious white spots, children with fillings/crowns completed within the past 2 years, children with gums that bleed easily, children with dental appliances such as space maintainers.

Other risk factors include: poor oral hygiene, inadequate fluoride, putting your child to sleep with a bottle or sippy cup which contains juice, soda and milk. Frequent consumption of high sugar foods like candy, cookies is also another risk factor.

3. HOW DO YOU TREAT FOR CAVITIES?

There are many different treatments for cavities. The most common ways of treating teeth are fillings and crowns.

Fillings can be metal or plastic. Metal fillings are called amalgams. Amalgams have been used as a filling material for over 100 years. Its advantages are that it takes less time and is less technique sensitive to place. It costs less than plastic ("white") fillings. It has a long history of success. In recent years the controversy about amalgam has been its mercury content. There has been no conclusive study showing negative health effects of amalgams. The disadvantages of amalgam use are that it requires removal of more of the tooth structure to place and it is not bonded to the tooth.

Plastic or composite fillings are tooth-colored, therefore giving a more natural look. They are bonded to the teeth, therefore allowing less loss of tooth structure when placing.

Some types of composite fillings release fluoride. However composite fillings are more expensive than amalgam fillings.

A crown is a cover placed over the entire tooth and is shaped like a tooth. It is used for teeth that are badly damaged or decayed. It is one way to treat severe tooth decay. If decayed teeth are not treated, the infection can spread in the mouth, leading to pain and other health problems. Crowns can be placed on front and back teeth. Pre-formed stainless steel crowns are the most common crowns used in baby teeth. Because the crown covers the entire tooth, it protects it from decay. Once the baby tooth is lost, the crown goes with it. For permanent teeth more durable crowns are recommended such as porcelain crowns, porcelain to metal crowns, all metal crowns (an alloy of several types of metals) or composite crowns. The type of crown used depends on the location of the tooth, age of the child and extent of damage to the tooth.

4. HOW DO I HELP PREVENT CAVITIES IN MY CHILD?

The American Dental Association recommends that children see the dentist no later than their 1st birthday. Visiting the dentist at such an early age will help them become comfortable with the dentist and establish the good habits of regular dental check-ups.

Breastfeeding is associated with a lower risk of developing tooth decay compared with bottle feeding. Good dental hygiene habits should start before your child's first tooth. You should wipe your baby's gums with a soft washcloth after eating. Once teeth appear, use a soft toothbrush twice a day. Avoid using toothpastes with fluoride until your child is able to spit out and not swallow the paste (usually age 2-3). Swallowing too much fluoride toothpaste can cause permanent stains on their teeth.

When choosing a toothpaste for your child, choose one that contains fluoride. Dispense only a pea size amount on the toothbrush. The type of toothbrush your child uses is important because the wrong kind can damage the gums. Toothbrushes should be made of soft nylon bristles and have a small head. The size of the toothbrush will increase as your child gets older. Toothbrushes should be replaced every 3 months or when they begin to look worn. If your child has had a cold or flu, replace their toothbrushes immediately. Electric toothbrushes can also be used with the same parameters. Both manual and electric toothbrushes work fine as long as they are used properly. Some parents may prefer electric toothbrushes because they encourage their child to brush longer.

Using irrigation devices such as a Waterpik is not necessary with children unless as an adjunct in children who wear braces. Irrigation devices do not remove plaque that is attached to a tooth. Plaque can only be removed manually (i.e., using a toothbrush).

Using mouth rinses should not be used on children younger that age 5 to avoid swallowing the rinse. Mouthwashes are used to freshen breath, whereas fluoride rinses coat teeth with fluoride, which helps prevent tooth decay. Fluoride rinses are recommended for children over the age of 6 as long as they know how to spit out the rinse. It is highly recommended for children at high risk for tooth decay.

In addition to brushing, flossing is very important to your child's dental health. You should start flossing your child's teeth as soon as they start touching each other. Choose the type of floss that makes the process easiest such as floss holders in bright colors.

5. HOW IMPORTANT IS FLUORIDE?

Fluoride helps make teeth strong by hardening the tooth enamel. Many cities have fluoride added to tap water. If you live in a rural area or an area where the tap water does not contain fluoride, your doctor may prescribe fluoride tablets when your child is 6 months old. Many of us drink bottled water instead of tap water. Bottled water may not have enough fluoride, which is important for preventing tooth decay and promoting oral health. The FDA and EPA ensure that the water we drink is safe and regulates bottled water as a consumer beverage. The FDA does not require bottled water manufacturers to list the fluoride content on the label, but it does require that fluoride additives be listed. If the bottled water contains from 0.6 mg/L to 1.0 mg/L, it may reduce the risk of tooth decay. If the fluoride content is not listed on the bottled water, contact the manufacturer.

With this in mind, if you drink bottled water with no fluoride, will that lead to more cavities? The answer depends on many factors which include the amount of fluoride your child receives from toothpaste, mouthwash, water, food and professional fluoride treatments. Other factor include how often and well your child brushes their teeth, flosses and what they eat and whether they get regular dental care. If you drink non- or low-fluoridated bottled water exclusively and are not getting enough fluoride from other sources, you may get more cavities than you would if you drank fluoridated tap water on a regular basis.

6. IF MY CHILD DOES GET A CAVITY, DOES IT HAVE TO BE TREATED?

Generally speaking, the answer is yes. Tooth decay is an infection. If a baby tooth is decaying, this infection may spread to other teeth and affect adult teeth when the child gets older. Infection in the teeth as with the rest of the body can affect your child's overall health.

Baby teeth start falling out around age 5 but continue up to age 12. Premature loss of these teeth can lead to shifting of teeth and loss of space for the permanent teeth. This is because baby teeth act as space savers for the permanent teeth. If baby teeth are damaged or destroyed, they can't help guide permanent teeth into their proper position. It is always easier to treat a cavity when it is small, in many cases with minimal or no local anesthetic, than when the cavity becomes large, painful, or the tooth becomes abscessed. At this point, the procedure becomes more involved, the prognosis decreases and the potential for early tooth loss increases. If your child has premature tooth loss, a space maintainer can be fabricated to hold the space open for the permanent teeth.

7. HOW DOES THUMB SUCKING AFFECT MY CHILD'S TEETH?

It is normal for children to suck their thumbs, fingers or pacifiers. It is a normal response to stress and anxiety. It does not mean that your child has emotional problems. Most children grow out of this habit on their own by age 4 with no permanent damage to their teeth. If your child is still sucking their thumb/fingers/pacifier after age 4, tell your dentist. This is because thumb-sucking creates a negative pressure in the mouth that has negative effects on the development of the face, flaring of the teeth, and a narrowing of the dental arches. These effects can last a lifetime.

In order to break the habit, some try home remedies such as painting bitter or spicy tasting liquids on the nails and fingers, wearing thumb or finger guards, or gloves. These methods occasionally work, but for the most part are not successful due to the instinctive nature of the habit. Parents can try educating their child on this behavior and pointing it out to them, but do not obsess over the behavior or ridicule your child.

Another option to stopping the habit is using a device called a tongue or finger crib. This appliance is "fixed" to the roof of the mouth, which means it is worn at all times. This appliance usually stops the habit almost immediately. This appliance is fabricated by the Orthodontist at a modest cost. The effectiveness of the "crib" lies in the fact that it removes the gratification of the habit. Crib wires prevent the thumb or finger from touching the roof of the mouth. After about 2-3 weeks you will notice improvement in the position of the teeth.

The best time to start treatment using a crib is when the baby front teeth become loose, usually around age 6. This treatment can also be used for teens and adults.

Healthy teeth are important...even baby teeth. Children need healthy teeth to help them chew and speak clearly. And baby teeth hold space for adult teeth. We need to do all we can to ensure that children get a healthy start.

About Dr. Isioma Anizor

Dr. Isioma Anizor is a General Dentist who practices in Lawrenceville, Georgia. She treats both adults and children in the practice she shares with her husband. They have two daughters. Her commitment to her practice is ensuring that even her youngest patients have a wonderful experience, setting them up for a lifetime of good oral heath habits.

Dr. Anizor grew up in Toronto, Canada and graduated from the University of Western Ontario with a Bachelor of Science in Biology. She then went on to graduate with a Doctorate in Dental Surgery from the University of Detroit Mercy in Michigan.

Dr. Anizor has extensive post-graduate training in many advanced and high-tech dental techniques, including pediatric dentistry, cosmetic dentistry, and restorative dentistry. She has taken hundreds of hours of continuing education. Her professional interests include pediatric and cosmetic dentistry. Dr. Anizor is a member of The Academy of General Dentistry.

Dr. Anizor's personal interests include travel, foreign films, music and reading.

Dr. Anizor can be reached at Optima Dental: (770) 962-4322
Or: www.lawrencevillefamilydentist.com

CHAPTER 13

BIOMIMETIC DENTISTRY

By Dr. Scott Stewart

Biomimetics - "Design by Nature" is an art/science which studies nature (the life form) in order to reproduce (mimic) nature's engineering into modern, naturally inspired man-made design. Designs from nature are applied to solve problems in engineering, materials science, medicine and other fields.[1]

National Geographic, April 2008: "Biomimetics" presented numerous examples of how science is closely examining our natural resources to revolutionize modern day life. Examples include a microscopic discovery of the 'tiny hooks' on the end of the spines of a cocklebur which biomimetically evolved into "Velcro" with hook and loop construction that grips instantly but lets go with a tug. (Now as common as the zipper.) Translating whale power into wind power - biomimetics helped design turbine blades with tubercles like the fins of the humpback whale. The scalloped edges of the fin help it generate force in tightly-banked turns. Wind turbine research utilizes this design to try to make more power at slower speeds than conventional blades, and with less noise. Biomimetics – mimicking design by nature - allows the use of a completely different set of tools and ideas[2] of natural, common sense origin.

---

1. Sydney Parker, a leading proponent of biomimetics, research fellow at the Natural History Museum in London and at the University of Sydney. Adapted from *National Geographic Journal*, April 2008

2. Michael Rubner, MIT, adapted from *National Geographic Journal*, April 2008

<u>Biomimetic Dentistry</u> utilizes this "different set of tools and ideas" along with modern materials and methods to restore natural strength, durability and health to damaged teeth. This method requires much less tooth reduction (minimally invasive), and utilizes the natural engineering of the tooth as a blueprint for its reconstruction. Our architect is Nature's original design. Our goal is to restore and maintain the health of the tooth for a lifetime. I like to think I'm 'rebuilding back to factory specs'. Not surprisingly, we are finding that biomimetic tooth restoration has eliminated the necessity for most root canals! It is our passion, as Biomimetic dentists around the world, to keep your teeth healthy for a lifetime utilizing nature's own design!

I've been in dentistry for nearly 29 years. It's a wonderful profession and I've enjoyed my choice of careers. However, after approximately 20 years of "drilling and filling," I became frustrated with the convention (insanity) that I had to "drill the tooth down" to a nub in order to "restore it" with a crown. This means removing all the enamel (the hard stuff) from the tooth, leaving just the inner dentin (soft stuff) remaining – major trauma to a tooth! Once you remove the enamel, it is gone forever and it does not grow back. The enamel in combination with the dentin represents the strength, resistance and durability of the tooth to everyday function - chewing and grinding food.

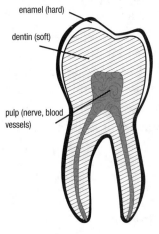

enamel (hard)
dentin (soft)
pulp (nerve, blood vessels)

You see, nature's combination of a thinner layer of hard enamel surrounding a large inner structure of soft dentin is the perfect design for total long term strength and breakage resistance.

Microscopically, this **'hard' and 'thin' fused to 'big' and 'soft' allows for give and flex** when under normal bite pressure ($200+$ lbs/in^2). **This is Nature's perfect <u>shock absorber</u>**. The protocol of conventional dentistry ("crowning") utilizes cement as the binding factor to cover very softdentin with an extremely hard and unnaturally thick "crown" or "cap". As long as the crown and cement grip the soft dentin stump, the system will function. If the cement fails, which happens, it's a real problem. Furthermore, an x-ray cannot 'see' through a crown to evaluate this situation. A major issue is (near-invisible) <u>recurrent decay</u> underneath the crown where the cement has failed allowing bacterial contamination. If this is found early enough, the crown can be removed, decay eliminated and a new crown re-cemented (more trauma). If not, the problem progresses to tooth failure, which means a <u>root canal</u> or <u>loss of the tooth</u>. Realize, if one gets lucky and finds the decay early, the <u>natural tooth stump</u> that remains after another necessary drilling event is now <u>even smaller</u> and <u>the crown gets bigger.</u> The cement then assumes an even greater role in the success of the new crown - not good! Add a root canal to this scenario and you now have a hugely compromised tooth with a questionable future! The risk for total failure goes way up and a significant number of these teeth will eventually require extraction and replacement. This is a costly and disappointing situation for the patient and for me as the dentist…well, it is not how I want to provide dentistry to the people who come to me for dental care.

So, I was *frustrated.* Frustrated with grinding the enamel off the tooth. Frustrated with exposing that much dentin. Frustrated with the sensitivity of the exposed tooth. Frustrated with the temporary plastic crowns required while the crown is being made. Frustrated with re-cementing the temporaries that come off while the crown is being made. Frustrated with having to re-anesthetize to put the new crown on. Get the picture? I was not happy with any of this process! Furthermore, many of the teeth that I was preparing for a crown had **significant portions of perfectly good enamel that were sacrificed because of the crown-preparation process.** *I tried newer techniques that left some of the enamel intact,* but I still struggled with having to temporize the tooth for another cementing appointment as I have mentioned above – with all the inherent frustrations.

Maybe I was lazy, didn't give it enough practice time to master all of the technical difficulties ... I don't know, but this just wasn't helping me to be a happier dentist. Frustrated as I was, with no further acceptable alternatives at the time, I resigned my ultimate quest for freedom...and returned...(sigh) to grinding enamel... and cementing crowns.

The next thing that happened hit me hard! My hygienist let me have it…right between the eyes. She was *absolutely disappointed, couldn't believe* I had made so much progress with 'partial crowns' (= preserving some of the enamel) and had reverted to my 'old enamel stripping ways.' I mean I really upset her! I didn't realize the impact of what I had previously touched upon. That is… **a more conservative, less invasive, enamel saving** crown-like preparation. She told me how much healthier patient's gums were when full crowns were not utilized and how much happier patients were that we had saved more of the natural tooth. She challenged me with how an enamel-saving technique "just makes more sense!" She then added, "why would you ever go back to your old ways when you were on the right track?" Well, she was absolutely right! I felt awful - I had let myself down as well as my team and my patients. I had verbalized a commitment to seek new ways of restoring teeth and I had "dropped the ball." I was still an "**enamel killer.**"

As fate may have it. Just a few weeks later, in 2004, while attending a dental meeting comprised of like-thinking friends and mentors, I was alerted by a good friend and fine dentist (Dr. Val Kilmer) that there was a fascinating 'out-of-the-box' dental technique just made available **that eliminated the need for crowns.** He related that he had just taken the intensive, multiple-day course, and offered me a glimpse at his notes. He was 'giddy' with excitement! I was beyond myself… this may be just the ticket I was searching for! I called the instructor, David Alleman, DDS - Center for Advanced Adhesive Dentistry/ Biomimetics, and enrolled immediately over the phone.

The Advanced Adhesive Biomimetic course was intense! Concepts backed by current and highly relevant science were beyond the "conventional box" of my previous education. My mind exploded with the possibilities! This was a huge 'benchmark' in my career as I finally had the go-ahead strategies and protocol I had so desperately been seeking to cure my 'enamel-killing' ways. Midway through the course work I called my hygienist. I told her that *if even half of what I was experiencing was true, it would change everything!* **Believe me - it changed everything**!

As of this time, during nearly 8 years since my introduction to Biomimetic Dentistry, I can proudly say that I have not ground down a tooth for a crown. The number of sensitive teeth, root canals and failures has been reduced to nearly non-existent. Biomimetic restorations are minimally invasive, enamel preserving, beautiful, life like and long lasting. Stepping it up a notch, these restorations can be completed in <u>one appointment</u>. This eliminates temporary crowns, sensitivities and issues stemming from multiple appointments and delay when having a conventional crown fabricated. I have an intense feeling of satisfaction when doing these incredible restorations! My patients tell me this is the best dentistry they have ever received – they love it! I feel I have a huge platform to brag, not of myself, but of the new/advanced technology that has turned my career and my world around. This is the very best solution for healthy and sensible restoration of teeth (not to mention better gum health) for a lifetime. I have this technology in my mouth, as do my team, my family and my patients. We will never go back - **Biomimetic Dentistry is here to stay**! **My ultimate thanks and appreciation to Dr. David Alleman for helping me open up a whole new world for myself and my patients!

BONUS: (*shameful secret exposed*) **Amalgams (silver or blackish metal fillings) **contain abou**t **50% mercury**! It has been proven that high levels of toxic mercury vapor are released when amalgams are removed – up to 100 times the maximum level allowed by government regulatory agencies. Make sure your dentist is "mercury-safe" with proper training utilizing specific "mercury safe" protocol and specialized equipment to safely remove amalgam mercury. *Don't be fooled*. "Mercury free" means that no mercury-containing materials are used for teeth restorations. "**Mercury safe**" means that if a mercury / silver filling is removed, it is done with prescribed and stringent techniques and equipment. This terminology is often improperly interchanged in marketing of dental services. "Mercury free" does <u>not</u> imply that a dentist is "mercury safe"!

For additional information see:
www.lakewoodbiomimeticdentist.com

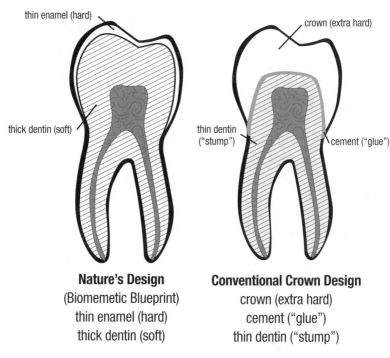

Nature's Design	Conventional Crown Design
(Biomemetic Blueprint)	crown (extra hard)
thin enamel (hard)	cement ("glue")
thick dentin (soft)	thin dentin ("stump")

Just say "no" to crowns

My *"Biomimetic Pitch"* to YOU, the **public....**

Do you have old dentistry that is falling apart, cracked teeth or have been told you need crowns? Are you seeking another choice? Would you like a less invasive approach? Would you like to prevent root canals and tooth loss if possible? Is *prevention* important to you? These questions come from statements made by people just like you who are looking for a better way to preserve and keep their teeth. Until recently, the "dental cycle" went like this ... filling ... bigger filling ... then a crown... then a root canal ... extraction ... implant... or eventually dentures if enough teeth are lost! Sound familiar? I hope not for your sake, but this comprises dentistry's top six treatment modalities!

There is a better way! What if we could "rebuild" a tooth using materials that look and act just like a natural tooth? What if we could save the healthy parts of the tooth and only remove and rebuild the parts that were damaged? What if we could microscopically seal that tooth so no bacteria could get inside again? What if we could do this in just one appointment?

"What if" is here now! Biomimetic dentistry is here – we are doing it in my office every day and have been doing it for almost 8 incredible years. Our patients tell us this is the best thing they have ever done for their teeth. Experience demonstrates that teeth restored in this way are far less likely to progress to abscess, root canal and possibly eventual extraction. The cost for this therapy is the same as a crown. Which would you rather have?

ADVANCED ADHESIVE BIOMIMETIC DENTISTRY – WHY WOULD YOU CHOOSE THIS?

With crowns/caps, there is considerable and needless loss of healthy tooth structure. The tooth is essentially reduced to a "peg".

With Biomimetics, there is little loss of healthy, supported tooth structure – only decay, areas of fracture / compromised tooth structure and problematic old dentistry are removed.

Crowns/caps rely on cement to hold them in place. This is a weak link with risk for leaking, further decay and infection. Once the crown is placed, tooth parts under the crown cannot be evaluated visually or by x-ray.

A Biomimetic restoration is sealed from the inside – out, eliminating pathways for bacteria to re-enter the tooth. This greatly reduces/eliminates the incidence of infection/root canals and further decay. A tooth restored this way can be examined both visually and with x-ray.

Crowns / caps have edges that sit on or near the gums making cleaning / maintenance more difficult and increasing the risk of gum problems and tooth decay. These 'edges' are also the cause of "dark line" seen around the gum area of many crowns.

A Biomimetic restoration does not have 'edges'. In most cases the area around the gum is not involved in the restoration and remains natural tooth. This is much easier to maintain – less risk for cavities / better gum health – and the esthetics are natural.

The rigid construction of a crown/cap prevents the natural flex and function of a healthy tooth. Many crowns are fabricated with metal or ceramic frameworks. When a "rigid" crown is put on top of a "flexing" tooth, the risk for failure increases –abscess, root canals, extraction.

A Biomimetic restoration is constructed in "fused layers" using materials that mimic the natural properties of the tooth structure – flex, expansion / contraction and shock absorption. This allows the tooth to continue to function as it was meant to. No metals/ceramics are used.

In many cases, a temporary crown is placed for a number of days until the permanent crown is fabricated. A second appointment is needed to fit the crown and cement it.

A Biomimetic restoration is most often completed in one appointment – no temporaries. A bite refinement may be needed the next day.

About Dr. Scott Stewart

Born and raised in Pawnee City, Nebraska, Dr. Scott Stewart completed his general education at the University of Nebraska and his dental training at the University of Nebraska Medical Center. Following completion of his doctorate, he attended 2 more years of internship in Tennessee and Ohio.

Dr. Stewart has trained with some of the dental industry's leading innovators and researchers. For those who want top quality cosmetic dentistry, Dr. Stewart has the training, expertise and experience of the Las Vegas Institute as well as the Kois Center of Advanced Dentistry behind him. For the latest in tooth preservation and restoration, Dr. Stewart has trained extensively with the Alleman Institute of Advanced Adhesive/Biomimetic Dentistry. Dr. Stewart is certified with the World Clinical Laser Institute for use of Waterlase™ and the diode laser. He is also trained and certified for the diagnosis, treatment planning and placement of Mini Dental Implants for tooth replacement and denture retention. His office is <u>mercury free</u> (no materials containing mercury are used) and **<u>certified mercury safe</u>** (safe removal of amalgam following protocol with specialized equipment). Dr. Stewart is trained and authorized for use of Medical Ozone. He is certified for the use of Conscious Sedation.

Professionally, Dr. Stewart is a member of numerous organizations including: American and Colorado Dental Associations, serves as a Delegate to the Metro Denver Dental Society, Academy of General Dentistry, Academy of Biomimetic Dentistry, American College of Integrative Biological Dental Medicine, International Academy of Oral Medicine and Toxicology, American Academy of Anti-Aging Medicine, International Association of Mercury Safe Dentistry, Academy of Laser Dentistry, Society of Global Mini Implants, International Association of Mini dental implants, World Congress of Mini Dental Implants, American Academy of Ozone Therapy, Dental Amalgam Mercury Solutions (DAMS), American Academy of Oral Systemic Health.

Dr. Stewart is a past chairman of K.I.N.D (Kids In Need of Dentistry) and served (chairman) with the Board of Delta Dental Insurance of Colorado. He is proud to acknowledge his membership as a Mason (32°) and is active as an El Jebel Shrine Clown. He is also a member of the Professional Colorado Clown Association.

CHAPTER 14

Dental Fear?
Fear No More!

By Dr. Edward T. Dougherty, Jr.

Everybody has a major fear of something. This fear may be about an activity such as flying or heights, a critter like a spider, perhaps being alone in the dark or a multitude of other situations or objects. The most universal response people have is to avoid the things they fear. This may work well in most instances, but what if your fear is going to the dentist? It is generally accepted that the fear of going to the dentist ranks among the top ten most common fears. Half the population will avoid going to the dentist on an annual basis. It is not uncommon for people to wait many years without receiving necessary care because of dental phobia. In my practice, new patients have usually postponed care for three to twenty years, but many have been without dental treatment well beyond one's imagination.

Avoiding the dentist, unfortunately, allows small problems to become much larger. A small cavity might require a simple filling but if neglected will continue to grow. If the decay approaches the tooth nerve it can become infected causing considerable pain. The once small filling becomes a larger filling, a root canal or a crown. Given enough time, this ever-increasing decay may lead to the loss of the tooth. Similarly, the gum tissue, which has an initial localized infection, if left unattended, can lead to progressive bone loss and eventually to loss of some or all teeth. The patient is now faced with the need for more extensive and expensive care to replace these missing teeth. The additional pressure for more treatment and expense adds to the fear and furthers the avoidance of care. The cycle continues over and over.

Dental neglect does not only cause physical problems, but rather takes its toll on our emotions. I have met many new patients who are very embarrassed because of their unhealthy mouth. Some have lost self-esteem because they feel they have "allowed" themselves to develop avoidable problems. Other patients are ashamed to show their teeth. With front teeth missing or blackened by decay, they avoid smiling or maneuver their lips so they do not show their teeth while speaking. Still others will shield their mouths with their hands to avoid showing any glimpse of their teeth. In extreme cases, a patient does not ever leave their home except for necessities.

From where does this fear, of receiving dental care, arise? I have observed five major categories as a basis for this phobia. The largest group of fearful patients can relate back to a bad experience at the dental office. For some, this may have occurred in early childhood and they have been living with these memories for their whole life. I have often been told by patients about being held down in the chair and crying while the dentist hurt them. Others describe the dentist who "had his knee in my chest" while attempting to pull a tooth. Some patients recall that every time they went to the dentist, they always seemed to require extensive care. Regardless of the veracity of these memories, they are very real and vivid for that patient and those memories keep them from seeking care. These apprehensions are also reinforced and compounded by friends, siblings and parents who seem ready to share their dental fears.

The second most common cause of this fear arises from the failure of local anesthetic injections to completely numb a patient. As with all other drugs, anesthetics do not work 100% of the time in 100% of patients. Fortunately, there is a wide variety of different local anesthetics and an array of injection techniques that allow the dentist to achieve almost 100% success. Unfortunately, once a patient has experienced the pain from not being completely numb, they never forget. One of my patients explained that he had no particular fear of dental procedures, but that his previous experiences were not always pleasant because he was not completely numb. Quite simply, he did not mind the actual procedures but did not want to be hurt. Who can blame him?

People avoiding the dentist because of a strong gag reflex comprise the third group of fear patients. These patients often have no fear of the dentist at all, but cannot tolerate things being placed in their mouth. The response to care may be a mild gag or a powerful reaction that ends in vomiting. Fortunately, a combination of sedation and auxiliary drugs can attenuate this response and allow a person to receive their necessary treatment.

The fourth group of patients is one that tears at your heartstrings. These patients have suffered sexual abuse. One male patient in his thirties advised me that when he was ten years old, an uncle had orally raped him over the course of a year. Another patient, a female in her fifties, told me that when she was young, a family member would cover her mouth and nose with his hand until she passed out and then would rape her. The positions a patient and dentist assume during care invade the "personal space" of an individual and can be quite threatening. Whether the horrific experience was rape or other trauma, it is easy to understand why these victims would not be comfortable laying back in a chair and having a stranger put things in their mouths.

The last major group is comprised of those patients with either physical or mental disabilities that do not allow them to receive care in a routine manner.

What assistance can be provided to all those who dread a visit to the dentist? The most important first step is to find an office where the people and the environment allow you to feel relaxed. Often, this alone may not be sufficient, and more help is needed to surmount this latent fear. For these patients, the various modalities of sedation are essential. The three most utilized approaches are nitrous oxide, oral sedation medications and intravenous (IV) sedation.

Nitrous oxide ("laughing gas") is a gas that is mixed with oxygen and inhaled through a small mask that fits on your nose. After breathing normally through your nose for a few minutes, the effects of the gas can be felt. The goal is to make you feel relaxed and comfortable. Some patients report feeling a bit light headed or having a tingling sensation in their arms or legs. This drug modality is not intended to put you to sleep. During the process you can communicate with the dentist and be able to respond to directions and requests or ask questions. The effects of the gas wear off after a few minutes once administration is completed and the mask is removed. Nitrous oxide is best suited for patients with only mild anxiety. An advantage to this type of sedation is your ability to perform normal functions after a brief waiting period, unlike other forms of sedation that put you to sleep and require you not to drive for twenty-four hours. The use of nitrous oxide is fairly common and so it is relatively easy to find a dentist who provides this service.

The second method of sedation is achieved by taking oral medications prescribed by or dispensed by your dentist. These drugs will have a more profound sedative effect than nitrous oxide. The quantity of drug is controlled by the dentist so that you remain awake but very relaxed and calm. This conscious sedation technique is best suited for mild to moderate anxiety. The dentist will have you either swallow a pill or let one dissolve and be absorbed under your tongue. In approximately an hour or less, the effects of the drug will be felt. The patient may become quite drowsy but will still be able to respond to directions and requests. The drug may diminish your memory of the dental procedures. The patient cannot leave the office alone after this type of sedation. You must not drive or operate dangerous equipment for twenty-four hours after being sedated but will be able to return to your normal activities the following day. Another potential downside is that the sedative effects of the drugs can diminish during the dental procedures. This is attributed to the different rates at which drugs will be metabolized in different patients.

The third form of sedation is intravenous (IV) sedation. This is considered to be the gold standard by which all other forms of sedation techniques are compared. The technique employs a small flexible catheter that is placed into a vein usually on the back of the hand or in the arm. Because the catheter is so small the patient rarely feels the insertion. A line is then attached through which the sedation drugs are administered. The drug is administrated in small doses (titered) until the desired level of sedation is achieved. Because of the precision involved in the dosing, many consider this to be the safest and most predictable sedation experience. Drugs administered in this manner are more effective than the same drugs given orally. The patient is very comfortable throughout the dental treatment. Most of the IV sedation drugs cause amnesia and so the patients are not aware of their care and feel like they were sleeping throughout the entire visit.

Dentists who administer IV sedation have received special advanced training in hospital programs. They are evaluated by their State Dental Boards who will certify them based upon their training, credentials, training of support staff and medical equipment available in their office. Because of the advanced, specialized nature of this technique, few dentists provide this service. A listing of those trained in IV sedation can be obtained through the State Dental Board.

The need for sedation-trained dentists is well beyond the availability of this care. It is my hope that sedation dentistry training will become more readily available for professionals serving the over 50% of the population that say, "I hate the dentist".

HOW TO FIND THE RIGHT SEDATION DENTIST – 10 SUGGESTIONS

- **When should I look for a sedation dentist?** The simple answer is before you need one. My experience is that most fearful patients wait until there is an emergency dental need. The emergency pain or infection has finally motivated them to seek care. Unfortunately, trying to find a stranger with whom you will be comfortable when you are afraid and in pain merely adds to the fear.

- **Is the dentist qualified to perform sedation dentistry?** All states require dentists who perform sedation to have a special permit from their State Dental Board of Examiners. Ask the dentist if he has one and check with the State Board. Some dentists will prescribe a minor tranquilizer (which is permitted) and then claim to be a sedation dentist (which they are not) in their advertisements and websites.

- **What type of sedation training does the dentist have?** Dentists who are trained to provide IV sedation have had extensive training in a hospital-based program. These programs are very comprehensive requiring extensive operating room experience. Dentists who provide oral sedation only receive on average three days of education in a non-hospital environment. The most popular of these programs is provided by the Dental Organization of Conscious Sedation (DOCS). It is also important to ask if the support staff is trained in ACLS.

- **How often does the dentist provide sedation?** Some dental practices are focused on meeting the needs of a sedation patient. In these offices, the dentist will be providing sedation services daily and develops considerable experience. In other offices a dentist may only occasionally provide this service in response to a patient's request.

- **What type of sedation does the dentist offer?** The various routes of administration have been previously discussed. They included IV sedation, oral sedation and nitrous oxide. The individual needs of each patient will determine what is appropriate, and therefore which office meets their needs.

- **What type of dental services does the dentist provide?** Be certain the dentist you chose is trained in the services that you need and performs them on a regular basis. You do not want to awaken from a sedation appointment and be told you will need to go to another office because the dentist was unable to provide a particular treatment.

- **Continuing education program?** Do not hesitate, during your interview of the dentist, to ask how often they and their staff receive recurrent training and continuing education in anesthesia. The fields of pharmacology and medicine are constantly changing and all doctors need annual training to remain current.

- **Is the patient a child or adult?** Sedation anesthesia is different for children and adults and the training required for the doctor is different. Again, match the dentist's training to your needs.

- **How do I find a sedation dentist?** First step is to call the Dental Board of your state. They will have on file a list of dentists with sedation permits. Next, go to the web and search for "sedation" or "sleep dentists." Here you will be able to find web sites for sedation practices. You will also find some websites that publish patient evaluations and comments about their dental experiences.

- **How do I begin?** Finding a dentist who understands your fears and anxieties will make you feel more comfortable. You can ask to schedule an appointment to meet the dentist without having any care provided. This gives you the opportunity to determine if you are comfortable with the doctor, the staff and the office environment. (Be prepared to pay a small fee for this visit). If the office thinks this is a weird request then move on, as this office will not be right for you.

Dr. Edward T. Dougherty, Jr.

www.DelmarvaSedationDentistry.com

Tel. 410-213-1482

About Dr. Ed Dougherty

Dr. Edward T. Dougherty, Jr. is known as "The Sleep Dentist" on the Eastern Shore of Maryland and the entire Delmarva Peninsula region. He is the dentist that patients turn to for help with their dental fears and anxieties. Local dentists refer their patients to him for those requiring the special services of sedation dentistry.

Dr. Dougherty received his training at the Johns Hopkins University, the University of Virginia and the University of Maryland. Prior to entering private practice, Dr. Dougherty served on the full-time house staff of the Johns Hopkins Hospital. He received his anesthesia training at the Montefiore Hospital in New York and St. Joseph's Hospital in New Jersey. His implant surgical training was undertaken at the world-renowned Misch Implant Institute. He received his advanced dental cosmetic training at the prestigious LVI Institute.

Dr. Dougherty was awarded the highest recognition of "Diplomate" by the International Congress of Oral Implantologists. This award is based upon extensive studies and patient case presentations in advanced dental implant and bone reconstructive surgery.

Dr. Dougherty has lectured nationally and internationally on the subjects of sedation dentistry and emergency medicine. He has been heard regularly on WMAL radio and interviewed frequently on WQMR radio. He has been seen on NBC news and his sedation practice has been the subject of articles in the Washington Post. He was voted the "Best Dentist" in the Washington, DC metro area by readers of the Bethesda magazine. Dr. Dougherty was recently featured on the nationally syndicated TV Show, The Ultimate Makeover.

Dr. Dougherty maintains a private practice of IV Sedation Dentistry in Ocean City, MD. He serves as an examiner for the Maryland Board of Dental Examiners evaluating dentists who apply for sedation permits. He is also an Adjunct Professor in the School of Dentistry at Loma Linda University.

Dr. Dougherty is an active member of the American Dental Society of Anesthesiology. The ADSA is an association of more than 5,000 members in the

United States, Canada and abroad. Dr. Dougherty is recognized as a Master in the College of Sedation Dentistry. This honor has been bestowed on only 145 members of the ADSA.

He annually travels nationally and internationally to provide charitable care to some of the most needy citizens of the world.

To learn more about Dr. Edward Dougherty and how sedation dentistry can help you overcome your fears so that you can achieve good dental health, visit: www.DelmarvaSedationDentistry.com or call 410-213-1482.

www.DelmarvaSedationDentistry.com

CHAPTER 15

Custom-Fitted Mouth Guards

By Raymond A. Mascolo, DDS

One of the biggest challenges we face as dentists is to convert our patients' needs to their wants. The other challenge we face is to be able to pay our bills each month. Sometime these two can work together but not necessarily in the ways that the practice management specialist will tell us. We have all taken courses in which the lecturer tends to put everything into a dollar amount. What is the value of not having to see a patient who has just received a concussion, and has had severe trauma done to their teeth due to not wearing any mouth guard or a minimally required mouth guard. We all know that contact sports require some type of helmet or mouth guard for protection. There is, however, a tremendous difference among mouth guards.

Dentists have a very high trust rating among the public. I think we have earned this rating and most of us hope that the people that are in it just for the money and are greedy would choose a different field. I personally became involved with making the *Drufomat pressure-laminated mouthpiece* when I became the team dentist for the NYPD boxing team. Most of the players were wearing mouthpieces that they had purchased in a local sporting goods store. Some bought the more expensive ones that are put into hot water and form into your teeth. Occasionally, we would find ones made by a dentist made by the Omnivac, which heated up a layer of plastic, and vacuumed stretched it over a model of teeth. Although fitting better than the other variety of mouth guards, there was a great inconsistency of the fitting over the teeth. While using pressure, the Drufomat provides a very consistent thickness and can also be multi-layered making it even stronger. Patients that have been wearing these mouth-pieces have stated that they are extremely comfortable and they fit well. (They are not playing with them in their mouth during their activity.)

I was instructed in the technique when I was attending the Academy for Sports Dentistry annual convention in Miami, Florida. The company Raintree-Essex was very cooperative with me when I began my study. They were very interested in the mouth guard survey that I conducted, and provided me with a lot of material. I also began to use a different type of alginate to make the impression for the mouthpieces. This new material again made by Raintree-Essex is a much better quality alginate, which mixes automatically in an auto-mixer. Since Raintree has been taken over by a larger company, I have not had much contact with them although I continue to use their products. Making the mouth guards is also a relatively simple job. Once a cast is made it is heated and pressurized in the Drufomat machine. After determining that the Drufomat technique made an excellent mouthpiece, I then tried to figure out why people do not find much value in owning them especially with the extensive list of injuries one can sustain to the oral-facial region.

What exactly are some of these injuries? Dental injuries can vary from a class one fracture of enamel to a class two fracture of the dentin, a fracture of the enamel and dentin, a fracture involving the pulp, and a fracture involving the root. Some people sustain total tooth avulsion, which requires hours in a dental chair with the possibility and development of other dental problems. Further injuries include laceration of the gingiva and contusion or abrasion of the gingiva or mucosa.

All these injuries also require a specific treatment, which can be very costly. In enamel fractures, treatment can consist of the minimum of smoothing and polishing of the affected area and in some cases binding or veneer work to replace lost tooth structure. Depending on the extent of the damages in a fracture involving the dentin, which is the second layer of tooth after the enamel, the patient might require an expensive bonding procedure, veneer or crown. In an injury involving the pulp, the patient would require a root canal treatment, core and crown. A root fracture or tooth avulsion would require the extraction of the tooth and a replacement, which includes either an implant or a bridge. In younger children, a dental injury can become even more problematic. Besides the obvious physical effects, studies have shown that injuries sustained to the teeth can have psychological effects on the children. In the case of a young child with an undeveloped root, an apexification treatment would be needed before a root canal can be performed. When a tooth is traumatized at an early age, the trauma does not need manifest itself instantly but can have implications when the child is grown. Teeth that are then replanted can become non-vital requiring a root canal at a later date. Teeth that are severely traumatized may also slowly die and may lead to infection.

As one can see, the injuries that can be sustained are quite severe. During my hospital training at Georgetown University, I personally replanted many teeth and treated dozens of mouth injuries. None of the patients were wearing a mouth protector. I have seen many of these injuries in my private practice, and again, none were wearing a mouth guard. The disparity of the scenarios of injuries that can occur is very serious. Concussion often causes significant and sustained neurophysiological impairments and psychological trauma. I understand that many accidents that occur are unavoidable, however sports injuries affecting the mouth can be greatly reduced by wearing a mouth guard. According to the US Health and Service Department, studies suggest that 39% of head and face injuries are sport related. The National Youth Sports Foundation for the Prevention of Dental Injuries reports that orofacial injuries are the most common injuries sustained during sports. It is estimated in the United States that there are 6 million athletes participating in high school sports per year. The likelihood of experiencing a concussion while playing a contact sport was estimated to be 19% during year of play. According to a December 2007 article in the Journal of Athletic Training, more than 62,000 injuries sustained each year occur in contact sports. Currently, these figures have been updated to reflect over 1 million concussions in the United States on an annual basis. Why then do people participating in sports not wear mouth guards?

In a study conducted through Adelphi University in Garden City, NY (where I teach tooth structure and dental terminology), we issued a survey to over 2000 Saint Anthony High School students and their parents. The results are as follows. Approximately 71% of the surveyed children participated in school sports. 78% of the parents also indicated that they had participated in school sports during their childhood. The majority also participated in organized sports outside the school. 67% of the children participated in organized sports outside of school while 69% of parents also noted that they had participated in organized sports outside of school. The majority of the children were not required to wear mouthpiece in the sports they participated in and only 32% reported that they were required to wear some mouth protection. Approximately 15% of those surveyed knew of someone who had a concussion or who have experienced a concussion themselves. 17% of children received a concussion from playing a sport while 22% of parents had received concussion from sports. 77% of the parents and children knew of some who had received a concussion. 62% of those surveyed knew of someone who had received a dental injury. 53% of those surveyed knew that a properly-fitted mouth guard could prevent a concussion. 73% knew that a properly-fitted mouth guard could prevent a dental injury. 61% of parents and athletes knew that mouth guards could be made with better fits and with other techniques. Only 18% of the athletes owned a dental mouth guard however, but only 20% thought it was comfortable. 57% thought that a custom mouth guard made by a dentist was too expensive. 25% believed that it would be over $100, while 35% believed it would cost $50-$100 and finally, 40% believed it would cost $25-$50.

It seems to me that the major reason mouth guards are not being purchased is that there is a perceived notion that they are expensive and are not of good value. This however is rather shocking. It is especially shocking considering how much people spend on athletic shoes and equipment, but forego protection for their teeth. When asked what they paid on average for athletic shoes, the answer was $120 per pair. The average spent on athletic equipment and league fees was $815 per year. The sad part is that people believe that spending $150 for a pair of sneakers is a lot, but $50 for a mouthpiece has no value. Unfortunately, we do not have the advertising power of Nike, Reebok or Adidas and the superstar athletes demonstrating how great their performance is enhanced by wearing these athletic shoes. It would be great to see a football player coming off the field showing how their mouthpiece (properly fitted) has improved their performance and kept them from receiving a concussion or dental injury.

According to Andreasen and Stevens, a properly-fitted mouth guard must hold the soft tissues of the lips and cheeks away from the teeth – so that laceration and contusions of the soft tissue during impact can be avoided. It must also cushion the anterior teeth and redistribute the forces from a direct frontal blow, fill in the space of missing teeth, and help prevent neurological injury by separating the condyles from the base of the skull during impact, reducing the intracranial pressure and bone deformation. It should also help prevent neck injury and prevent opposing teeth from coming into violent contact. A properly-fitted mouth guard will provide the athlete with confidence that they are less likely to sustain an injury, giving them the competitive edge for aggressive competition.

I feel that it is our responsibility as dentists to educate the public to the value of custom-made mouth guards. It is clear that the public has been misinformed. Getting back to the financial aspect of dentistry, mouth guards can give rise to a new market for dentists. As mentioned previously, I am the team dentist for the NYPD boxing team. I have found that quite a few of these people who do not have a dentist of their own became my patients. They were so impressed with the quality of the mouth piece that it made them realize that they would receive quality dental treatment under my care. Patients who had their own dentists were routinely returned back to that dentist for care. Since over 50% of people in this country do not go to a dentist, there is a vast market of patient resources that we have access to. I purchased the Drufomat machine to make the mouthpieces and this has lowered my overall cost. I feel if I can provide my patients with high-end mouthpieces and possibly prevent a concussion or serious mouth injury, then I am fulfilling my duty as their dentist. Many patients are grateful for this service and I believe it strengthens the bond between my patients and myself. I know people who charge $300 for mouth pieces such as mine, and many people are reluctant to spend that much money especially in these hard economic times. Having people wear the mouthpiece is also a good source of referral to the office, because it gives an opening to speak about the excellent dental care they received. Patients normally don't bring up their dental experience, (other than in the form of a complaint) unless they feel it is special. Providing a custom mouthpiece is just something special I can do to show my patients how much I care about them.

In conclusion, I do believe that organized dentistry must take a more active role in making patients aware of the advantage of a properly-fitted mouth guard to prevent dental injury and concussion. It is also my opinion that dentists should try to make these appliances available to their patients at a reasonable fee. People will not be able to know the value of the mouthpieces until they have used them. I had a patient who lost his maxillary lateral incisor while playing basketball – taking an elbow to the mouth. I remember seeing him on a Sunday morning right after this happened. Since he is very concerned with his appearance, he did not want to go to work missing his front tooth. After oral surgery was performed I bonded a temporary tooth. Subsequently, we restored the missing tooth with an implant. After this, I made him one of the custom mouthpieces, which he wears routinely now whenever he plays sports. It is a hard thing to know that if I had gotten him to wear the mouthpiece, this could have been prevented. It is very hard at times to convince people to do what is good for them. I know that this patient has told his story to many people and very few people think it will ever happen to them. As these mouthpieces become more popular, I believe many more people will begin to wear them and greatly increase the market for them.

One of the fighters for whom I recently made mouthpieces had not seen a dentist since he left the US Army. Whenever I watched him box, he was constantly moving his store- bought mouthpieces around in his mouth. When he was fighting, he would have to clench his teeth to keep it from dislodging. This also made it difficult for him to breathe. After I made him the new mouthpiece using the Drufomat technique, he informed me that it greatly improved his boxing technique – since he was not concentrating on keeping the mouthpiece in place. He stated that the mouthpiece was so comfortable that he did not even realize it was there, and it also allowed him to breathe much more easily.

I also believe that there is a market for this type of mouthpiece in law enforcement and I have begun to make the mouthpieces for special units in the police department. Members of the SWAT teams and Corrections Officers who are constantly involved in physical contact when dealing with criminals and unruly in- mates, can greatly benefit from this appliance.

We, as dentists, are very honored to still have an excellent rep- utation with the public and are still able to treat our patients for the most part as we desire. Helping our patients out with low-cost, high-quality mouth guards is another way of saying 'thanks' to our patients.

About Dr. Raymond Mascolo

Raymond A. Mascolo, DDS received his dental degree from Georgetown University Dental School in 1980. He completed a general practice residency at Georgetown Hospital. He has been in private practice since 1981 and has been practicing at his current location since 1988. Dr. Mascolo serves on the faculty at Adelphi University in Garden City, New York both as an adjunct professor of Biology, teaching "Tooth Structure and Dental Terminology," and director of the Pre-Dental Preceptorship program. He was a founding member of the Adelphi University Dental Advisory Board and has been affiliated with the School's joint degree program with Georgetown and Tufts Dental Schools.

Dr. Mascolo serves as a police surgeon with the Suffolk County Police Department and has been the team dentist for the NYPD and Suffolk County Police Department boxing teams. He served as the commander of the 4102 FMST with the NY State Guard from 2002 to 2006. He has received many awards for his community service and has been named Man Of The Year by several organizations. Dr Mascolo is in the Hall of Fame at both Archbishop Molloy High School in Queens and Saint Anthony's High School in Huntington. He has completed training in weapons of mass destruction awareness and has completed 32 FEMA courses. He was part of a disaster mission during hurricane Katrina. He currently serves as Vice President of the Police Surgeons Benevolent Association and as President-elect of the Dentists for a Better Huntington. He has been very active with helping homeless veterans and devotes much of his time to this cause. He can be reached at: Cptmasc14@aol.com.

CHAPTER 16

The Miracle Of Sedation Dentistry

By Dr. Ramin Moradi

There is no denying the incredible advances made in modern dentistry in the past several decades. What was considered impossible just a few years back has become very predictable with today's materials and methods. One of the biggest changes in today's dental office is the manner in which the patients themselves are treated. It wasn't long ago when patients felt they were at the mercy of the dentist, and unfortunately, the dentists weren't doing much to change that perception. As a result, we now have several generations of people who list going to the dentist as one of their least favorite things to do. The latest reports claim 31% of baby boomers never go to the dentist; or only go in an emergency. 75% of U.S. adults experience some degree of dental fear. 15% of the population declines necessary dental treatment because they fear oral injections. This is something that was robbing millions of people of a healthy mouth and all that modern dentistry had to offer for years. Fortunately, a very simple, yet extremely effective solution was on the horizon.

Triazolam is a simple pill which allows the patient the opportunity to have his or her treatment performed while sedated, leaving them feeling completely at ease. Classified as a sedative-hypnotic, it is in essence a sleeping pill, which has as an added benefit, the ability to give the patient amnesia for the few hours he or she may be on the medication. Having treated hundreds under this technique, I, along with the patients treated, would list sedation as a true game-changer. Most of these patients have a story to tell as to what made them weary of going to the dentist, or worse, stop going all together. Most will also tell you how choosing sedation changed not only their oral health, but also helped change their very being.

David was 53 years old when he conjured up the courage to visit my office for the first time. A pleasant middle-aged man with a quick wit and a quicker smile, we had become fast friends. All was going well until we got around to the subject of dentistry. It quickly became apparent that he was not very comfortable being in the chair. If it was not for the toothache he had been fighting for the past few months, this would be the last place you'd find David on a Wednesday afternoon. Just a simple examination turned into quite the ordeal for him. Sweating, palpitations, and stuttering took over the exterior of a calm, cool gentleman. Despite our attempts to convince David of modern day dentistry and the benefits of conscious sedation, it would be a couple of years before we heard from him again.

When I got a message to give David a call, he told me he would like to "try again." He claimed he was always a good patient by most standards. He came from a modest background, yet his parents insisted he visit the dentist every six months. This had become his routine most of his young adult life up to the point when he joined the armed forces at the age of 18. This, according to him, is when things took a turn for the worse. Having been a regular when it came to visiting the dentist, he was at ease going into his dental check up at the military base. After all, his family dentist had been telling him he was doing a great job and that all looked spotless every time he'd been in for his 6 month check up for the past few years. It was for this reason that what he was about to hear from this "amateur technician" was a total blow to everything he had been doing to keep his pearly whites perfect. Twelve cavities! And to top it off, four wisdom teeth that needed to go! His initial thought was to wait until he sees his own dentist and get reassurance that this was all a mistake and that all was just fine – just as he had been told repeatedly in the past. Unfortunately, this would not be happening. David was told that this is the way that it is, he will need to get this dental work taken care of here and now, and that was it. "The more I tried to fight it, the worse it got", David explained. "To top it off, we were all just beginning to know one another at the base, and the last thing I wanted to do was look like the wimp!"

I could hear how this was tearing David apart some thirty years later! It was like it'd just happened yesterday! David went on to explain how helpless he felt as he slowly relented into letting the 'butchers' have their way with him. "They were ruthless! I told them I could still feel everything! I cried, I screamed, I fought, all to no avail! It was like a bad nightmare, yet I couldn't wake from it! After a while it seemed like I was having an out-of-body experience! This couldn't be me - this couldn't be happening to me! It was as if I was zoning out, trying to salvage what little dignity I had left in me." When all was said and done, some four hours later, David left with a very sore mouth. The pain in his mouth, according to David, was nothing compared to the pain he felt inside. The tooth pain eventually subsided, but the pain and the scars left inside would not be so easy to overcome with the pain meds.

As the years went on, visiting the dentist became more and more of a cause for fear in David. He would use any excuse not to go. If and when he did go, it was for an absolute emergency when all else had failed. To make matters worse, the dentists he visited made things worse, calling him a "wimp, a coward, a terrible patient." It seemed no one could understand him; as if he was the only one to have ever had such an experience – David felt all alone. The once pearly whites had turned yellower and yellower as the years continued. Cavities formed, chips appeared, and teeth were lost. The once ever-present smile of an extrovert became more and more one of a recluse. He stopped taking care of the rest of him as he could not see the purpose in it all. "What's the use in combing my hair, in wearing clean clothes, in keeping up with the rest of my hygiene, when my mouth looked like a train wreck?!" David's own family couldn't understand what was happening to him. Whenever David tried to explain what had happened to him, he was met by everything from "that was so long ago," to "just get over it!" Seeing that no one seemed to get just what he was going through, David found it easier just not discussing 'it'. Unfortunately, that seemed to drive him further and further into depression. Modern medicine wasn't much help either. "All they wanted to do was get me on more drugs! I wasn't sick, all I needed was someone to understand where I was coming from!" Unfortunately, that day was still 'a ways' away.

I was visiting the neighborhood book store when I met David for the first time. As the store manager, he took it upon himself to see that no questions went unanswered for his patrons. A very professional and cordial man, he was very easy to feel comfortable around. When the subject came up, I informed him that I was a dentist in the area. I could immediately tell by his body language that he was another 'dental case' from the baby boomer generation. I seemed to have put his mind at ease by sharing with him that most every patient I have seen in his age group has a dental story to tell, for he asked for a business card. I continued to run into David from time to time at the bookstore, and every time, he would tell me how he needs to make that appointment soon. I never pushed, and it would be a good six months before I saw his name on the schedule.

David was scheduled as my last patient of the day for a consultation. We gave him plenty of time to tell us his story as well as all his expectations. Once finished, with his permission, we started our examination. Starting with the x-rays, to the clinical exam, to the impressions of his mouth, we continually asked for feedback on anything we could do to make things as comfortable as possible for him. Our goal was to have him feel like he was in absolute control of the situation. In addition, we gave him plenty of breaks along the way in order for him to catch his breath. This was, after all, the first time he was seeing a dentist in what seemed like forever to him. Even more amazing was the fact that he was actually getting into it all. He was slowly beginning to see that what he had feared was maybe not quite as bad as he may have thought.

The news was not good. There was too much bone loss to consider saving any of his upper teeth. In all, he would have to extract nine upper teeth. He had a couple hopeless teeth on the bottom arch, along with three, which would need root canals and full coverage crowns in order to save. In addition, he had several other teeth that would need extensive restorations, and ten implants to restore his mouth back to optimal dental health. The good news was that he could have all of his treatment performed in the same office under conscious sedation. "A simple, safe, yet extremely effective pill, which would allow you to be absolutely comfortable while all your dental treatment is completed." It's what David had been waiting for all these years. He would be in and out of sleep for a good part of the day, while his dental health would be brought back from years of neglect. Considering the price tag, I told him that we could give him several options from the best, to what would suffice. Surprisingly, he informed me that if he was to do the treatment, he wanted the "Rolls-Royce" treatment. He did want some time to let everything sink in before making any final decisions. We told him that we would be available for any additional questions at any time. We did follow up with a couple phone calls as well as a letter just to let him know that we were always available without meaning to sound too pushy.

Finally, almost a couple years later, when I had just begun to think we had seen the last of David, we got the phone call. He was finally ready to do it. He needed the time to get everything into place before committing to it all. He had read up on sedation dentistry and realized it was everything he needed. A visually more confident David was ready to be in charge. He came in, got his financials taken care of, picked up his medications and was told to be here the following Saturday morning by 8 a.m. for a nine hour appointment. I think this was the most excited I had ever seen David.

David was driven to our office by 7:45 that Saturday. Visually drowsy, we took him to our sedation operatory, got him comfortable in the dental chair with a soft pillow and a warm blanket, got all our monitors in place, and saw David drift into a very comfortable state. It was a long, challenging appointment, but everything went over seamlessly. It was 4:30 in the afternoon when I informed David that we were done. While still groggy, he seemed perplexed at what I was telling him. "What do you mean I'm done?!" asked David, rubbing his eyes together. "You're all done! You did great!" I told him excitedly. "What are you talking about?!" David asked, now raising his voice a bit. "Everything went great! Your ride is here to take the new you home!" I told him, while handing him a mirror. His look was priceless. He just kept looking at the mirror, without saying a word. After a few moments, he cleared his throat and muttered "You are a magician!" The assistant and I had a laugh over it.

Speaking to David, the night of the appointment, I was happy to hear that all was perfect. It is truly amazing how much psychology is involved in the pain aspect of dental treatment. This is something I have seen over and over in treating patients under sedation. The fact that they are not totally conscious while the treatment is taking place, it's like nothing happened at all! David had just about every type of dental procedure performed on him during his appointment; from surgical gum therapy followed by laser debridement, to extractions, implant placement, crown preparations and root canals. Not only was he totally comfortable during the procedures, he really felt no pain or discomfort afterwards either. He credited us with his recovery, but I know it would have been next to impossible to get him there was it not for the sedation. An added benefit to Triazolam is the fact that the patient also doesn't remember most of what happened during the appointment!

David has gone on to share his story with everyone. He has come to look forward to his dental checkups again, and excited to see us on his recall visits.

The top three reasons to consider sedation dentistry today are:

1. Anxiety. A few decades back, dentists alienated themselves from the rest of society by making themselves out to be these heartless practitioners. As a result, there are literally millions today who are terrified of going to the dentist.

2. Time constraints. Even with all the technology and benefits of living in the most modern society, we are busier than ever today. Finding the time to go to the dentist can get pushed down to the bottom of the list for many people. To be able to perform multiple procedures in just one sitting can be very attractive to most patients.

3. Disabilities. Mental or physical disabilities can make sitting in a dental chair for multiple hours very difficult for some. I was able to see a patient with a bad back for nine hours without a single problem due to the sedation procedure. Prior to that appointment, he had a difficult time sitting in the chair for more than twenty minutes without his back acting up.

There are so many other reasons to consider sedation dentistry that it could easily fill up the rest of the pages of this book. Patients with a high gag reflex do fantastically well with sedation. Patients who salivate a lot are great candidates for sedation since it helps curb the saliva temporarily. It is such a safe and effective drug that it has opened the door to countless people who had all but given up on dentistry and their oral health. I truly feel blessed to be part of an amazing profession where I can help transform someone's life through the amazing advancements available in today's dentistry. What Sedation Dentistry has managed to do is to open a door that may have been closed to so many more deserving people.

About Dr. Ramin Moradi

Dr. Ramin Moradi is a graduate of the esteemed University of Southern California (USC) School of Dentistry, and the recipient of an AEGD degree from University of California, San Francisco (UCSF).

Dr. Moradi is an experienced practitioner with a true passion for bringing the very latest dental innovations to all his clients. Numerous postgraduate programs have given him a broad base of knowledge in areas covering most of what is relevant in dentistry today. From full mouth makeovers and CAD-CAM dentistry, to the latest in Sedation Dentistry, Dr. Moradi and his highly-trained team have been successful in treating numerous patients in Northern California for the past fifteen years. Dr. Moradi has been the recipient of several awards for the dentistry he has performed throughout the years.

Dr. Moradi can be contacted on: Me@DrMoradi.com.

CHAPTER 17

The Facts About Bad Breath and Bad Health:
The Breakthrough That Could Save Your Life

By Greg Rubin, DDS

Bad breath. It seems like such a silly little problem. Maybe it causes a little social discomfort and that's all. That's the fiction.

But the facts are much more alarming. Bad breath, aka "halitosis", can actually be a symptom of an underlying medical condition. Increased health problems, such as strokes, osteoporosis, infection of the bones, heart attacks, diabetes, pneumonia and premature births are all linked to bad breath and it's underlying cause, periodontal (or gum) disease.

Surprised? Most people are.

More than 30 million Americans (some research suggests: up to 80% of all adults) experience bad breath - and most of them aren't even aware they have it! As a practicing dentist, I may be more aware of it than most people, since I'm looking in their mouths on a daily basis. But I've also studied more than most. I founded and developed the first-ever halitosis treatment center in 1987 - and I now help other dentists set up their own treatment centers as well.

Bad breath isn't silly - as a matter of fact, it can be an extremely serious signal of larger health problems. In this chapter, I'd like to discuss just what causes halitosis - and the exciting break-through I've discovered that can conquer it once and for all.

WHAT'S BEHIND BAD BREATH?

First of all, everyone gets bad breath occasionally, and tempo-rary bad breath is not a big deal. You can easily get short-term halitosis from eating spicy or strong-smelling foods (and these are foods you can easily guess would be the culprit - onions, garlic, chili, etc.). Smoking or drinking alcohol can also cause bad breath.

You've also probably heard of "morning breath." Lots of people have bad breath right when they wake up. That's because saliva is supposed to be keeping your mouth clean, but it tends to dry up while you're asleep.

This kind of bad breath is relatively easy to dispose of. You might have something to eat that makes it go away, or, prefer-ably, you'll brush your teeth or rinse to get rid of the condition.

Unfortunately, sometimes bad breath doesn't go away with these quick fixes and it lasts throughout the day. That is a strong indicator that there's something else wrong that needs more than a quick fix.

Occasionally this kind of long-lasting halitosis is caused by a medical problem somewhere else in your body. For example, sinusitis, which is an irritation in the spaces formed by the bones around your nose, or tonsillitis, when your tonsils become in-flamed due to viruses or bacteria, can both cause it. Even heart-burn can cause stomach acid and gas to travel back up your throat and create bad breath.

Diabetes can also become a problem when it causes your body to burn fat for energy instead of glucose, causing your breath to smell fruity or sweet (this is a very serious concern and you should immediately seek medical attention if this occurs).

The overwhelming majority of the time, however, for 85 to 90% of those with bad breath, the condition is caused by the bacteria that live in their mouths.

BAD BREATH AND BACTERIA

Bacteria, if you didn't know, are tiny organisms - there are hundreds of kinds of bacteria. Some live in your body and never cause a problem. But some are harmful and, if left unchecked, can cause disease. In your mouth, if they are plentiful enough, they will grow and give off gases as they develop - these gases are what can make your breath smell bad.

What's the source of these gases? Well, bacteria, just like us, humans, eat food and excrete waste - it's a fundamental living process. The waste products produced by some oral bacteria are sulfur compounds. Have you ever smelled a rotten egg? Well, that particular stench is caused by a sulfur compound. In other words, sulfur compounds can create a pretty big stink.

And that's only the beginning, because the bacteria in our mouths produce other unique and unpleasant smells with their waste byproducts, which include:

- **Isovaleric Acid** - the smell of sweaty feet.
- **Skatole** - the smell of human excrement
- **Putrescine** - the compound responsible for the odor of rotten meat
- **Cadaverine** - the smell that makes you think of corpses

Yes, think about all that running amok in your mouth! Not very appetizing, is it? And the fact is that everyone has some degree of these nasty compounds in their mouths. But, when bacteria levels are low, the average person can't smell any of them. It's only when they grow beyond healthy levels that someone might wrinkle their nose at what's coming out of our mouths.

So where exactly is all this bacteria that's discharging all this -

excuse the expression – crap, in our mouths?

Well, one large breeding place is the tongue. And generally, the part perpetrating the bad smell is in the back. Go to a mirror and stick your tongue out. Look closely and many of you will actually be able to see a whitish coating on the tongue's surface. The further back you look, the whiter the layer. This is actually dental plaque, even though it's not attached to any teeth, and it's loaded with the type of bacteria that result in bad breath. That's why it's important to brush the back of your tongue; when the bacteria count is lowered, there is usually a direct correlation to an improvement in odor.

Another prominent place for bacteria to thrive is at and below your gum line. The area between the teeth and towards the back of your mouth tends to be a problem area. Even when your mouth is relatively healthy, these bacteria pockets exist - obviously, the worse the state of your gums, the more bacteria there are.

As I already mentioned, saliva is supposed to clean out your mouth so these bacteria don't grow to the extent where they can cause bad breath. There are other instances, however, where you may not be producing enough saliva to do the job. That may be a result of:

- Taking certain medications, such as antihistamines and certain antidepressants
- High blood pressure
- Not drinking enough water
- Not eating regularly enough
- Breathing through your mouth instead of your nose
- The salivary glands in your mouth not producing enough saliva
- But just as bacteria in your mouth are the primary cause of bad breath, the primary cause of bacteria in your mouth...is gum disease.

As all good dental patients know, gum disease is the result of plaque, which is a coating that develops on your teeth that's mainly made of...you guessed it, bacteria! These bacteria can infect your gums and make them inflamed, swollen, bloody and sensitive. That inflammation is the consequence of your body trying to protect you from germs - it's how the body tries to heal an injury or an infection.

Gum disease proceeds in two main stages:

- **Stage 1, Gingivitis:** In this stage, your gums will become red and swollen. When you brush your teeth, you may find they bleed easily. Gingivitis can be combated by brushing your teeth twice a day and flossing. A dentist or a dental hygienist can also give your teeth a professional cleaning.

- **Stage 2, Periodontitis**: This is a later and more serious stage of gum disease, in which your gums begin to pull away from your teeth and form infected pockets. If you don't get treatment for periodontitis, the bones, gums and other tissue that support the teeth can be destroyed. That could result in tooth loss, and cause very serious health problems.

The fact of the matter is that bad breath is also a sign of other health issues in other parts of your body - health issues that could literally be a matter of life and death.

HOW SERIOUS CAN BAD BREATH BE?

Research in the United States and elsewhere around the world has demonstrated that the condition of your breath reflects your overall health - and can be an accurate way to predict other health problems.

One researcher, Dr. Robert J. Genco, the editor of *The Journal of Periodontology*, discovered that heart attacks occur in people with decayed or decaying gums over 250% more than people with excellent oral health. As Dr. Genco wrote, "Among the sample group we looked at under the age of 60, gum disease was an even more important risk factor for cardiovascular disease than was high blood pressure."

What links heart trouble with gum disease?

Well, the mucous membranes in your mouth are full of antibodies. These antibodies, or immunoglobulins, protect you from viruses and bad bacteria. As we get older, our bodies produce less of these antibodies, so we have less and less resistance to the more than 600 different kinds of oral bacteria we carry around in our mouths each minute of each day.

A tear in the gum line can allow toxic oral bacteria to flow into your bloodstream, into your arteries and into your brain. These bacteria can cause the walls of your arteries to expand, reduce the circumference of the blood vessel, and constrict it - which could lead to a potential heart attack or stroke.

Even mothers who are pregnant run the risk of premature births if they have gum disease and leave their bad breath untreated. Several reliable research reports show that expectant women with high levels of the bacteria that cause gum disease have *over eight times the risk* of delivering an underweight and premature baby

FINDING THE BREAKTHROUGH OF A LIFETIME

Obviously, after reading this chapter up to this point, it's easy to see how bad breath is not only a social embarrassment for those who suffer from the affliction, but can also be a serious health problem, depending on the severity and the cause of the halitosis.

This is why I've devoted most of my professional life to finding new and innovative ways to stop bad breath and destroy the powerful bacteria that is so often the cause. I wanted my patients to be able to keep their breath healthy for a lifetime. And by the way, it wasn't just my patients I wanted to help - it was also myself.

Yes, I suffered from bad breath. (In the beginning of my career...) I brushed and flossed even more than I tell my patients to do it - with no lasting results. I even had painful and expensive gum surgery to try and correct it. It's not fun speaking to your wife, kids, and friends and worrying about bad breath - not to mention my patients and my staff at my practice. I can also share with you some responses that I have heard from my patients when I asked them, if they had asked their dentist for help with the bad breath problem. What I heard was: "Dr. Rubin, I realized that I have A BAD BREATH PROBLEM....so I went to my dentist... and he smells worse than me... so I did not ask him about my problem

All my life, I've been waiting (researching and experimenting and studying) for an affordable, natural and healthy way to prevent bad breath for my patients. Well, it took over 25 years of research and study, but I finally found the solution I was looking for - and it also provides the amazing side effect of providing an enhanced immune system. I call it the BIOS Protocol™ (Bio Immersion Oxidation System), and I'd like to explain what it is and why it works for me, as well as the people I treat.

The BIOS Protocol™ is a patented system and custom device that is FDA approved, and utilizes a safe and natural compound that is prepared to my specifications by a special compounding pharmacy. There are no harmful chemicals; all ingredients are FDA approved - which means it's totally safe for people of any age. And because the material is so concentrated (we make it in a pharmaceutical grade), you only need to use a small amount - its effects are long-lasting.

You apply the BIOS Protocol™ to your gums, where it not only protects them against bacteria, but it also attaches to the receptor sites in the gum tissue and is absorbed into your bloodstream. It equips your teeth and gums with antibacterial material that they need to withstand the ever-present bacteria in your mouth.

The BIOS Protocol™ is exclusively available at my Calabasas Dental Institute in Calabasas, California.

We have patients flying in from all over the country.

HOW TO KNOW IF YOU HAVE A BAD BREATH PROBLEM

As I mentioned earlier, many people with halitosis are unaware they even suffer from the problem! I thought I'd conclude this chapter with some of the warning signs you need to look out for in order to detect if you might have a problem with bad breath.

Ask yourself these questions:

- Are people complaining about my breath?
- Is it difficult for people to discuss bad breath with me?
- Are people moving away from me when I speak?
- Are my gums tender, bleeding or easily irritated?
- Are my friends offering me gum all the time?
- Am I noticing a change in my love life?
- Are my teeth decaying?
- Are my teeth loose and getting looser?
- Am I suffering from a lot of sores in my mouth?
- Am I afraid I have bad breath and just don't know what to do?

Remember, bad breath can be successfully treated - I'm the living proof of that! If you'd like more information on bad breath or the BIOS Protocol™, I invite you to contact me at: drrubin@no2badbreath.com

About Dr. Greg Rubin

Greg Rubin, DDS is known as a "Halitosis Expert" and the creator of the Bio Immersion Oxidation System™. He has been in private practice since 1984 with the main emphasis on cosmetic dentistry and breath treatment. He specializes in the treatment of Halitosis (bad breath), utilizing FDA approved and patented systems, and has been treating patients with Bad Breath for the last 25 years.

Dr. Rubin founded and developed the first ever Halitosis Treatment Clinic in 1987 and has offered this unique and needed service to thousands of his patients since then. He also helps other dentists set up Halitosis Treatment Centers in Dental offices nationwide. Recently, after conducting extensive clinical studies, he developed a special protocol for dental treatment of patients with diabetes and other medical problems — known as "Dr. Rubin's Method of Dentistry".

Dr. Rubin's current dental practice utilizes a new FDA-approved technology to treat gum disease that is very common in diabetic patients. Everyone on Dr. Rubin's staff is trained to work with dental patients with special needs.

He is also an inventor, educator and consultant for dental manufacturers and holds a number of international patents in dentistry. In 2003, he founded the International Dentists Inventors Association (I.D.I.A.). This association provides assistance with product development, intellectual property and manufacturing outsourcing advice, and consulting with dentists that have new product ideas.

Dr. Rubin's multi-specialty practice also provides services of Implant Restoration and Cosmetic Smile makeover treatments at his offices: the Calabasas Dental Institute in Calabasas, California.

Dr. Rubin attended Jerusalem University Medical School (Israel) and received his Bachelor of Medical Sciences in 1981. He graduated in 1984 from Tel–Aviv University Dental School in Israel and is licensed to practice Dentistry in Israel, the United States and China.

Dr. Rubin is a former clinical instructor at the University of Southern California (USC) Dental School and University of Nevada (UNLV) Dental School.

MEMBERSHIPS AND ASSOCIATIONS:

- Member of American Association of Dental Examiners
- Member of ICOI - International Congress of Oral Implantologists
- International Dentists Inventors Association - Founder and President
- ADA - American Dental Association
- CDA - California Dental Association
- Alpha Omega International Dental Fraternity
- AAID - American Academy of Implant Dentistry